THE TACONIC TRAGEDY

A SON'S SEARCH FOR THE TRUTH

Written by Jeanne Bastardi

First published by Dog Ear Publishing
4010 W. 86th Street, Ste H
Indianapolis, IN 46268
www.dogearpublishing.net

ISBN: 978-145750-623-9

This book is printed on acid-free paper.

Printed in the United States of America

This book is dedicated in loving memory to

Michael Bastardi Sr.,

Guy Bastardi

& Daniel Longo

"You live in the hearts of those who love you."

And in loving memory of

Rachael Bastardi

Who was waiting to take them into
Her loving arms.

A Message from Michael...

There is no greater pain than having lost my father and brother from the senseless act of a drunk driver. My love for my father and brother, Guy, will continue to be as strong as it has been my entire life. This book is not only about the horrific acts of Diane Schuler and the suffering that she has caused so many people but also about the added pain caused by those who fabricated stories about her actions that day.

I was raised in an Italian-American family. My father taught me how important family is. I especially remember when he told me that my brother will "always be [my] brother" and that I should always be there for him—and that my brother would always be there for me. My brother was always there for me.

In keeping the promise that I made to my father, I hope this book can in some way speak for my brother, Guy, and my father. They are two of the greatest people the world will ever have known.

Michael Bastardi Jr.

Acknowledgments

A special thank-you to our children Taija and Isaiah, for tolerating the time it took to write this book and for sharing your thoughts and sorrows.

A sincere thank-you also to a*ll of our family and friends* for the support that you have given *all of us* and for the sorrow that you have shared; nothing and no one has been overlooked.

We would also like to thank the following people (listed in no particular order):

Phillip Amicone, Mayor, City of Yonkers, NY
The New York State Police and Investigator James Boyle
City of Yonkers Police Department, Precinct One
Emergency responders
The Funeral Procession Police Officers
American Legion Hawthorne, NY, Post 112
St John the Baptist Parish of Yonkers
Flynn Memorial Funeral Home
The Caring Public and the Residents of Yonkers

Table of Contents

Key People

Name	Importance
Michael Bastardi Sr.	died in Taconic Tragedy
Guy Bastardi	son of Michael Sr. /Died in Taconic Tragedy
Michael (Mike) Bastardi Jr.	Son of Michael Sr.
Jeanne Bastardi	wife of Mike Jr.
Taija Bastardi	daughter of Mike and Jeanne Bastardi
Isaiah Bastardi	son of Mike Jr. and Jeanne
Roseann Guzzo	daughter of Michael Bastardi Sr.
Bob Guzzo	Roseann's husband
Bobby Guzzo Jr	Roseann's son
Richie Guzzo	Roseann's son
Nicky Guzzo	Roseann's son
Margaret (Marge) Nicotina	daughter of Michael Bastardi Sr.
Joe Nicotina	Marge's husband
Joe Jr. (Joey)	Marge's son
Michael (Mikey) Nicotina	Marge's son

Danny Nicotina	Marge's son
Richie Nicotina	Marge's son
Jenna Nicotina	Marge's daughter
Christina Nicotina	Joe Jr.'s wife
Joseph (Joe-Joe) Nicotina	Joey and Christina's son
Brianna Nicotina	Joey and Christina's daughter
Diane Schuler	Driver who caused the accident on the Taconic Parkway
Daniel Schuler	Diane's husband
Joan (Jay) Schuler	Daniel's sister-in-law
Warren Hance	Diane Schuler's brother
Jackie Hance	Warren's wife
Irving Anolic	Bastardi family attorney
John Q. Kelly	Bastardi family attorney
Dominic Barbara	Daniel Schuler's attorney
Thomas Ruskin	Daniel Schuler's private investigator

1
Last Call

July 22, 2009

It was hot and sunny, a beautiful Wednesday. Mike, Jeanne, and their two children, Taija and Isaiah (Ike), were on the beach in Wildwood Crest, New Jersey, with Jeanne's sister Carolyn and her two daughters. A well-kept secret, the Jersey shore has some of the finest beaches on the Atlantic seaboard. The water was blue and stretched to the horizon, sparkling like a million diamonds. From his chair, Mike could see his son with his daughter and their cousins. Taija and Alexa were at the water's edge, and Ike and Amanda were riding the mini surf on their boogie boards. Mike's wife was asleep next to him on the beach blanket, and his sister-in-law was reading. He remembered that he had told his dad that he would call him. Mike's brother, Guy, had reminded him a few days before that, "Dad is still waiting for you to get someone to fix the gutter."

That's my father; if you say something, you have to follow through. Immediately! Mike thought, laughing to himself. This seemed like a good time, so he dialed his father's number. His father, Mike Sr., answered right away. "Hi, Dad; it's me, Mike."

Mike's dad told him that he, Guy, and their friend Dan Longo wanted to come up to Mike's house on Sunday and have a barbeque.

Mike reminded his dad that he and his family would not be leaving the shore until Sunday, so they planned the visit for the following weekend. They talked for a while, Mike's dad asking how everything was down at the shore, and Mike knew his dad was visualizing it as they talked.

Every year since Mike was a child, his family had gone to the shore together. Over the years, the family vacation had grown to include spouses and children. Mike's parents enjoyed having all the grandchildren together at the shore, and now there were two great-grandchildren. Mike assured his father that he, Jeanne, and their children would be coming back down to the shore when the family went in August and explained that he had already booked a room. He could tell that his dad was really looking forward to the August trip. Mike was still smiling when he hung up the phone.

2
Shattered

July 26, 2009

It was a beautiful Sunday in July, sunny and hot, and traffic was moving along nicely. Trooper Rosenthal was on duty in his patrol car. Things were quiet, and he was thinking about the end of his shift. *This should be an easy afternoon. I'll be home in time to enjoy a barbecue.* His thoughts were interrupted by dispatch. A wrong-way driver was traveling southbound in the northbound lanes of the Taconic State Parkway from the Pleasantville Road exit. He glanced at the clock: 1:30. With lights flashing and siren wailing, Rosenthal headed southbound at full speed starting at mile post 7.5, expecting that the driver would have realized the mistake and pulled over by now.

Meanwhile, witnesses watched in horror as a red minivan barreled down the parkway in the wrong direction. Neither honking horns, flashing lights, frantic arm-waving, nor cars swerving out of the way alerted the driver to her mistake. She stayed focused and continued to travel at a high speed in the passing lane of oncoming traffic.

Some witnesses could see children in the red minivan. Now, real danger…a curve. Rounding the slight curve in the road, the minivan found itself almost facing a black GMC, which quickly veered to the right, the driver watching in horror through the rearview mirror as the van rocketed head-on toward another oncoming SUV, a Chevy Trailblazer. The GMC driver held his breath.

The two vehicles seemed to explode as they hit. The minivan rolled down the hill and burst into flames. The Trailblazer was pushed across two lanes and was struck again by another small SUV, a Chevy Tracker. Stunned motorists stopped their cars on both sides of the highway and ran to the scene.

Another dispatch came through to Rosenthal, reporting that there had been an accident northbound on the Taconic near mile post 4.1. Trooper Rosenthal arrived at the scene within two minutes of the original call to find what appeared to be a red minivan engulfed in flames in the median. Trooper Rosenthal was immediately approached by a frantic motorist telling him that there were multiple fatalities, some involving children. The trooper radioed for additional EMS and fire support, advising that there were fatalities at the scene. As he grabbed the emergency kits, all thoughts of a barbeque ended.

Passersby stopped to help. They quickly pulled the surviving children out of the burning minivan and laid them on the ground. Some children had been thrown from the van and were lying about. Five children had been traveling in the minivan. People were grabbing blankets and first aid kits. Rosenthal began working on two little girls at the scene. They were unresponsive. Another little girl had a pulse but did not appear to be breathing; frantically, responders used breathing apparatus on her. Those with the stomach for it were checking the other vehicles. The screaming and crying rose above the din and chilled everyone who heard it. A passing paramedic rushed to the scene. He yelled to bystanders to move the victims farther away from the burning van. He examined the woman and two young girls and shook his head at onlookers; they were dead. A doctor from

Kings County Hospital came upon the scene. He joined in to examine the little boy, who, though lethargic, was kicking and screaming. The doctor suspected bleeding in his brain.

More people who pulled over approached the Chevy Trailblazer. Three men were trapped inside. One man tried to help the driver, holding his head. The driver opened his eyes, appeared to gasp for air, then closed his eyes and slumped in his seat. There was no way to get the men out.

Troopers Kirkland, Gonzalez, and Delaney arrived at the scene. Rosenthal observed the gray Chevy Trailblazer in the northbound lanes of the Taconic. Inside, he found three dead men. He looked into the third car, the gray Chevy Tracker that had also been involved in the fatal accident. He spoke to the driver and passenger in the Chevy Tracker. Both had sustained minor injuries.

The scene had quickly become chaotic as emergency workers started to arrive. Emergency crews from the towns of Hawthorne, Thornwood, Pleasantville, Briarcliff Manor, and Mount Pleasant reached the accident site. A female child from the minivan and both people from the Tracker were taken to Phelps Memorial Hospital. The boy from the minivan was taken to Westchester County Medical Center.

The accident scene was a disaster site. Responders placed a mat and an umbrella over two of the victims to shield them from motorists' views. Passing motorists continued to stop without hesitation to offer any help they could. New York State Police investigators Boyle, Becerra, and Morgan and Sergeants Muller and Kranik had arrived at the scene. Rosenthal assisted with scene security and obtaining witness statements. Control of the case was turned over to criminal Investigator James Boyle.

At 3:00 p.m., Boyle checked with Westchester Medical Center, which advised him that Brian Schuler, the male child from the minivan, was in stable condition. At the hospital, Boyle met with Warren Hance, whose sister, Diane Schuler, had been the driver of the minivan. Warren's three young daughters had been passengers in the minivan along with Diane's two young children, a daughter, Erin, and a son, Brian. The New York State Police had directed Warren to the hospital at approximately 2 p.m., after he had stopped in Tarrytown to seek assistance in finding his sister's van. Warren was aware that Brian was at the hospital but did not know the whereabouts of his sister, three daughters, or niece.

Though a veteran police investigator, Boyle had never gotten used to this part of the job. In one fatal second, a man had lost his three young daughters, his niece, and his sister. He notified Hance that his sister and the four girls had died. From the hospital, Warren notified his wife, Jackie, by phone, of the accident and of the deaths of their three children. Warren then notified Daniel Schuler, who was the father of Brian and Erin and the husband of Diane, of the tragedy.

Realizing the magnitude of the accident and the rising death toll, Investigator Boyle returned to the accident scene with that familiar uneasy feeling, an almost hollow feeling that makes your mind spin and forms a lump in your throat—the feeling that brings on a sudden desire to rush home and hold your own children tightly. He arrived back at the accident site to find Westchester County Medical Examiner's Office Investigator Michael Messinger on the scene, along with other members of his department. They removed the bodies of Michael Bastardi Sr., Guy Bastardi, and Daniel Longo, the three men who had been traveling in the Trailblazer, from the scene. With an entire wall of white tarps lined up, the officials from the medical examiner's office managed to remove the bodies of these men with privacy and dignity. Later, this would prove to be an enormous comfort to the victims' families. The medical examiner's investigators then approached the red minivan, a Ford Windstar that now appeared gray in color from the fire, where a dead woman, Diane Schuler, was lying on the ground under a blanket west of the vehicle. To the south of the vehicle were two of the dead little girls, Erin Schuler and Alyson Hance. Further south of the vehicle was another of the dead little girls, Emma Hance. The children were removed by the medical examiner's office investigators.

New York State Police Troop K Collision Reconstruction Investigators Shannon Alpert and Sergeant Larry Muller began their investigation at the scene.

****

Mike packed up the car and prepared to leave Wildwood. It would have been a great beach day, he thought, clear and hot. His wife, son, daughter, and a friend of his daughter all piled in the car. It was still early, so they stopped to eat outside of town. By 12:30, they were on the highway. Driving home, they hit traffic, so it was about 3:30 when they pulled up the driveway. It was always good to get back home. They all hurried to unpack the car, and Mike lit the barbeque. *Might as well enjoy the nice weather,* he thought. They were still settling in when the phone rang. Mike heard his wife say, "No, he's not here. We just walked in. Why, what's going on? Hold on, I'll put Mike on. Maybe he knows." Jeanne handed Mike the phone while explaining that it was his sister Marge, who had asked if, by any chance, his father was there.

Marge had spoken softly as she always did, so Jeanne had not really noticed the concern in her voice. Marge and her husband, Joe, lived near Mike Sr. and Guy in Yonkers, about an hour's drive from Mike's house.

Mike took the phone. "Hi....What do you mean, did I see him?" he asked.

Not sounding too alarmed, Marge explained that their dad, along with Dan and Guy, was supposed to have stopped at their sister, Roseann's, to eat but had still not arrived, Mike told her no, he had not heard from them. He knew that their father had a tendency to just show up unannounced, so it was not unusual for his sisters to think that their father may have gone to Mike's house first. Mike asked Marge to let him know when she heard from their father and Guy.

As soon as Mike hung up, the phone rang again. This time it was his sister Roseann asking if he had seen their father and brother. He told her that he had just spoken to Marge and that no, he had not seen their family members. Roseann sounded worried. Sensing that, Mike asked her what the problem was, and she informed him that they were very late and that no one was able to reach them on their cell phones. They should have been there hours ago and now Roseann and her husband Bobby were hearing that there had been an accident on the Taconic. Their father and brother might be stuck in traffic, but because no one in the family was able to reach their cell phones, they couldn't confirm. They knew that area was a cell phone dead spot.

A few minutes later, Mike's phone rang again. It was Mike's brother-in-law Bobby, Roseann's husband. Bobby said that the accident being reported on the news had fatalities and that one of the cars looked like Mike's brother's car. Mike did not really grasp what Bobby had said. He told Mike that he was trying to get more information and would call back.

Jeanne grabbed the house phone. Mike heard her ask the operator for the state police in the vicinity of the accident. She was connected and then redirected to a different office. Mike heard her give her name and ask if there was information on his family, stating that the news had said there was an accident with a fatality. She was transferred again, and someone took her name and number and told her that a detective would call her back. Jeanne's face was wreathed in concern.

The entire family started to panic.

Two hours passed very slowly, with a lot of uninformative phone calls coming in. Jeanne tried not to let Mike see the sheer panic she was in because his own panic was so obvious.

Joe and Marge were pacing their kitchen floor, stopping every few minutes to re-dial Mike Sr.'s home phone and then his cell. When Joe heard the house phone ring, he grabbed it. The caller ID showed his father-in-law's number, and his heart jumped. *They're home,* he thought, his heart pounding. *They had been caught in the traffic from that accident after all.*

****

Investigator James Boyle and Trooper Christopher Rachek drove to the home of Michael Sr. and Guy Bastardi to notify their family of the men's deaths. They found no one home but learned from neighbors that the two men lived in the house alone. A vehicle in the driveway was registered to Daniel Longo, with a different address. The investigators entered the residence through an unlocked garage door. While inside, Investigator Boyle observed numerous missed calls on the phone. From the residence, he phoned the number shown on the caller ID, which belonged to Joseph and Margaret Nicotina. When Boyle identified himself, Joe Nicotina asked if his father-in-law had been involved in the accident being shown on the news. Investigator

Boyle confirmed that Mike Sr. had been in the accident, and then he asked for Nicotina's address.

At 6:00 p.m., Boyle and Rachek arrived at Nicotina's address, where Boyle made the death notifications to Marge.

It had been a long day, and Boyle and Rachek still weren't done delivering tragic news to these families. Boyle wondered if sometimes this job was too damn stressful for anyone to take.

****

Mike's cell phone rang again. It was Roseann's husband, Bobby. He told Mike that the state police had been to Marge and Joe's house and given them the tragic news. Bobby informed Mike that Guy's Trailblazer had been involved in the accident and that Mike's brother and father and Dan had been confirmed dead at the scene. Mike did not remember much after that. Mike started yelling into the phone, "No way." It didn't register. "No way, it can't be." Jeanne asked him what had happened, but Mike was unable to speak. He just dropped the phone and walked outside, collapsing on the lawn.

Jeanne followed him, asking, "What happened, what happened?" Mike still could not answer. He could barely breathe.

Jeanne grabbed Mike's cell phone and called Joe. Joe was speaking calmly, but his voice was shaking, unusual for the big, rugged man. Joe told her that Dan, Guy, and Mike Sr. were all confirmed dead.

It was impossible to absorb. Not realizing that her daughter and son were watching, Jeanne screamed, "Which one, which one? It can't be all three."

The children started screaming and crying. Jeanne was still on the phone, repeating, "Everyone, all three? It's just not possible." As Mike lay on the grass, still unable to move, Ike was running around, bringing out water, towels, and Bayer aspirin. Ike was so confused; he was in shock.

Mike just lay there, trying to move, but unable to get his body to function. He still couldn't move. He was trying to absorb the impossible. Finally, after what seemed like hours, he got up. Still not understanding the scope of the tragedy, Mike called Joe back, trying to figure out what had happened, why it had happened, and how it could have happened. Joe explained that a woman had been driving the wrong way on the Taconic. As Joe spoke, Mike's face contorted in unbearable pain. It was hard to listen. The confusion was making his head pound. He walked back and forth. It was hard to focus. His stomach ached. Maybe it was a mistake. Maybe someone else was the fatality; it didn't seem possible that it could be all three, Dan, Guy, and his father.

Mike hung up the phone with Joe and called his longtime friend and attorney, Irving Anolik, who was really more like family. Mike gave Irving what details he knew. Irving tried to keep Mike calm and assured him it would be all right. Mike told Irving that he was leaving for his sister Marge's house in Yonkers and would keep him informed. By this time, the story of the accident, now updated with news of the fatalities, was hitting even more news channels. Mike walked inside to tell Jeanne that they had to leave and see the rest of his family. He had to find out more of the details, and he knew he had to be there for his sisters.

Jeanne called the cell phone of Pete Fiumefreddo, Mike's cousin. Pete had spent a great deal of time with Mike's dad. Jeanne had always seen them together, so Pete was the first person she thought to call. When Pete answered, she tried to tell him what had happened. It took several attempts before he could understand. He told her to take it easy, he would take over making the phone calls and would notify the rest of the family.

Next, Jeanne called her brother-in-law, Brian Magnotta. She knew her sister Carolyn and her nieces were coming home from the Jersey shore the next day. Jeanne didn't want to tell her sister when they had such a long drive. When Brian answered the phone and

Jeanne tried to tell him what had happened, he couldn't understand what she was saying, either. She had to repeat it several times. It was hard to talk, but it was also hard to absorb. Brian said he would get a hold of Carolyn. Of course, Brian was also afraid Carolyn would learn of the accident and the deaths on the news or that his daughters, Alexa and Amanda, would see it online, because he knew they would have their laptops on. His daughters had spent a great deal of time and several holidays with the Bastardi's, and he didn't want them to hear about the accident that way.

Jeanne had arranged for some of her family to come stay with her and Mike's kids; her mother and one of her sisters, were already arriving.

Mike and Jeanne left for Yonkers.

****

At approximately 8 p.m., Investigator Boyle spoke with Joseph Longo. Joseph confirmed that he was Daniel Longo's brother and he would be the next of kin for identification purposes, and Boyle officially notified him of Daniel's death.

After he hung up the phone, Boyle thought about the little boy, Brian Schuler. *Let's hope he makes it*, he thought. *There's been enough loss.*

Back at the Hawthorne state police headquarters, Boyle received a transcribed witness statement from Trooper Rosenthal. The report from Rosenthal stated that the witness "saw what seemed like two cars explode; the one car was on fire and went down a hill. He had tried to help the kids, a woman at the scene told him the van had been going the wrong way."

Boyle then interviewed a witness who stated that he had been "traveling north on the Taconic and exited at the Pleasantville Road exit, when he observed a red minivan enter through the same exit ramp, heading in the wrong direction. He stated that he honked his horn and waved at the vehicle but was ignored. He stated that the driver did not appear to be swerving in the road." The witness's passenger, his wife, confirmed his statements.

Investigator Joseph Becerra was also taking witness statements. One witness told Becerra that he too had been "coming off the Pleasantville Road exit and noticed a red minivan coming at him going the wrong way on the exit ramp." The witness told Investigator Becerra that he had honked his horn and waved, to no avail, and had had to swerve his car onto the shoulder to avoid a collision. Other cars, he said, had been doing the same. After pulling his vehicle onto the shoulder, the witness had observed the vehicle continue onto the parkway.

Investigator Becerra interviewed another witness who stated that he had been "driving north on the Taconic in the center lane when he saw a red minivan coming towards him in the left lane and that it appeared to be traveling at a high rate of speed. He did not see the vehicle after it passed him."

The statements were sounding the same but giving no insight into what had gone so terribly wrong. Why had the driver of the minivan continued to drive in the wrong direction with other motorists warning her? After entering the exit ramp and getting on the parkway in the wrong direction, facing oncoming traffic, why had she not pulled her vehicle off to the shoulder after realizing the mistake? Why speed toward oncoming traffic?

****

Mike would eventually remember leaving the house after receiving the phone call from Bobby, his wife driving and how quiet it was, sitting there and thinking, just hoping this would not be true, that he would get a phone call that his father, brother, and friend were alive. Thinking that by the time they reached Yonkers, it would have been a mistake, and that his family had survived. The anxiety during the one-hour drive was overwhelming, each minute, agony. He waited for the cell to ring, to hear there had been a mistake. As they drove, he pictured his father and brother. He imagined what they had seen, what they had felt. The drive seemed interminable.

As the car turned down the street to his sister Margaret's house, Mike saw his brother-in-laws and seven nephews standing outside. The reality started to sink in. He saw what was really going on here. Before him was a street full of sobbing men and boys.

Mike got out of the car. His brother-in-law Bobby grabbed him. They had grown up together, had known each other since boyhood. Their parents still lived on the same block. Until today, that is. Bobby had married "the girl next door," Mike's sister, Roseann, and they had raised three sons. Bobby knew how hard this would be for Mike. They looked at each other without a word.

Joe grabbed Mike next. They walked to the backyard to see Mike's sisters and the rest of the family and friends who had already gathered. The looks of shock and grief were unbelievable. There was an ominous silence. There was nothing to say. Seeing Mike, Roseann and Margaret fell apart. Constant sobs filled the evening.

An hour passed while all tried to get their thoughts together. "Someone has to go lock my father's house," Mike said. No one wanted to go. Jeanne volunteered and left for the house. Pulling up in front of the house, a terrible feeling came over her. She realized why she was there. Jeanne walked into the house and up the stairs. It was eerily quiet. She realized that she had never been in the house alone before.

As she reached the kitchen, she heard a knock on the door. Assuming that one of her nephews had followed her, she threw the door open. Standing there was a reporter wanting to verify the victims' names. Jeanne was stunned and called Mike's cell. How and why would a reporter even know to be here? It was 11 p.m. Mike told Jeanne to wait there, he would be right over.

Mike and the rest of his family jumped into their cars and headed over to the house. Within minutes, the cars pulled up. Looking at the house, Mike was overcome by a feeling of emptiness. The reporter was waiting outside; he seemed like a nice and sympathetic man, but Mike did not want to hear the word "victim" just then. He was still hoping the death notice was a mistake. He went into the house, leaving his brother-in-laws outside to speak with the reporter.

Once inside Mike realized the house just felt big and empty, and that was unthinkable. The sense of emptiness, loss, and pain was consuming his body. He went downstairs to the apartment that their father had fashioned for Guy. Mike found Guy's office, the room that they had shared as boys, and sat down. He watched the fish swim in the tank and looked at some notes that Guy had left that morning. He could hear Guy's laugh. Mike's head dropped and hit the desk. He could not comprehend the pain of loss he was suffering, and he walked around the apartment mindlessly. He was visualizing Guy there, trying to picture Guy sitting at his desk.

Mike went back upstairs. Memories of his father and brother overwhelmed him. He looked around at his family pouring out tears of grief, sobbing, wrenched in pain, but with no words to express their pain. Mike watched them from a distance, unable to recognize the grief-stricken faces.

Mike went down the hallway to his father's room. He looked at his father's bed and thought of how his father had just been there that morning. The feelings that consumed him were near unbearable; he kept thinking that this could not be happening. Nothing made sense.

Mike walked into his father's den and sat at the desk. He thought about how much his dad loved his computer, how he had sent emails and pictures to all of them. The kids all got a kick out of that. *He became very computer savvy after my mother's death,* Mike thought. He looked at the computer and found his father's telephone list. Neatly typed and listed in order by age were his children and grandchildren and their house phone and cell phone numbers. Mike kept thinking that his father would have to be coming home; this could not be the end. No, it could not end like this. He sat and waited for this nightmare to be over.

The television went on down the hall. Mike could hear the newscaster giving a few details of the accident. A woman had gone down the Taconic Parkway the wrong way, hitting another car head-on, and eight people were dead. The words hit him like an electric shock. He could not bear to hear that said out loud. He did not want to know it was true. He did not want the woman to tell the whole world. He was holding out hope that his family had survived, but at hearing there were eight dead, his hopes crumbled.

As he walked around the house, Mike realized that no one there seemed to be able to complete a sentence; they spoke with nods and single words. Three people were too much to lose at once. It was too much for any of them. How could all three be gone at the same moment? He looked at his nephews and niece, his nephews' wives, girlfriends, friends. They all looked so different now. *This is not my life*, he thought. *This can't be our family.*

It was late when Jeanne and Mike started the one-hour drive home to upstate New York. The drive back home was even quieter than the drive down. Still in shock when they got to their house, Mike just walked upstairs and collapsed on the bed.

3
The Reality

July 27, 2009

Monday morning, the Bastardi family woke up to news headlines about the accident. They had been given very few details by the police, so the news hit them fast and hard, headlines such as "Eight Die in Horror Crash" and "Wrong Way Minivan in Fiery Horror."

Mike wanted to leave for his father's house early and meet his family there. The drive down to Yonkers that morning was even harder than on the day before, and with the same silence. Mike felt like his entire world had just stopped. Thoughts of his father and brother swirled through his mind, not in any particular order...recent thoughts and distant memories, of conversations they'd had and some Mike had wanted to have. It was too painful to think about both his father and brother being gone. The thought of his father's funeral was hard enough. Trying to imagine his younger brother, his only brother, laid out next to his dad was unbearable. *My brother should be here to bury my father with me*, Mike thought. His thoughts were jumbled, and he couldn't concentrate.

When Jeanne and Mike arrived at Mike Sr.'s house—known by the family as Grandpa's house since Grandma had died—some of the family were already waiting outside, along with some reporters. Jeanne went up the steps quickly while Mike's brother-in-law Bobby came down to greet Mike. Looking at Bobby made reality hit Mike again. Mike was overcome by emotion; he felt his legs giving out. The next day, Mike would see himself on the cover of the newspaper being carried up the stairs, but he would still be too numb to notice or care.

Once inside the house, Mike and Jeanne saw an array of newspapers from different areas. The papers carried assorted pictures from the crash scene: pictures of state police, emergency crews, and the vehicles...vehicles that were no longer recognizable. Varying reports from witnesses and rescue workers told a story of total chaos and shock. One paper quoted a police source as saying, "The driver was screaming. She was on fire" and the chief of the Hawthorne Fire Department as saying, "This is the toughest scene I've ever had to cover." The fire chief said the driver and five others occupants, all kids, had been thrown from the minivan and lying on the ground, their bodies on fire: "I had five kids burning up and I had to make a decision."

Reading the stories forced all of the family into reality. Another paper quoted a witness on the scene as saying he had run up to the minivan and seen the female driver engulfed in flames. "It was too graphic... I don't even know if her legs were there." Another article in the same paper stated that stress management teams were being called in for the emergency responders. The Bastardi family was starting to see how horrific the accident had been and just how chaotic the scene had been. It was hard to imagine that their family members were part of this horrific crash; it was surreal.

Sitting at the kitchen table, Mike could hear the television on in the living room. The news anchors were all trying to make sense of this tragedy, speculating on how this woman could have been driving the wrong way on the Taconic Parkway with a van full of children.

One witness said, "We could see the minivan coming right towards us; it did not seem to swerve, or move into any other lane. It was deliberately driving in the wrong lane, in the wrong direction at a very high rate of speed. It seemed to be driving very deliberately in that lane despite people honking and flashing their lights at it."

When a New York State Police news conference came on, Mike and Jeanne joined the others already gathered around the television in the living room to watch. State Police Captain Michael Realmuto explained that the red Ford minivan had entered the Taconic Parkway at Pleasantville Road, going southbound in the northbound lane, and had traveled for 1.7 miles in the wrong direction before striking another vehicle, a Chevy Trailblazer head on and causing a third vehicle to hit the Chevy Trailblazer. At this point, the police did not know what had caused Diane Schuler to go the wrong way on the Taconic Parkway. Police were awaiting autopsy and toxicology reports, he announced. There was no reason at this time to believe Diane Schuler had been intoxicated or impaired by drugs.

Reporters asked if police thought Schuler had done this deliberately, and the police asked the reporters not to speculate at this time, explaining that it appeared Schuler had entered the ramp, and drove across three lanes of traffic to the left lane, facing oncoming traffic. She had contacted her brother two hours before to say she wasn't feeling well. It was still unclear what symptoms Ms. Schuler had been experiencing when she had contacted her brother from the road. "She called her brother because she just wasn't feeling well," said Lieutenant James Murphy of the New York State Police's Bureau of Criminal Investigation. "She didn't indicate specifically what was bothering her, but it was obvious something was wrong because her brother did ask her to pull over and state he would come up and locate her." Lieutenant Murphy added that, "She seemed a little disoriented and did not know where she was when she spoke to Mr. Hance."

Various news channels would replay the state police news conference all day but did not offer any answers, just more questions.

Mike and his sisters had to discuss funeral arrangements and select a funeral home so the funeral home could pick the bodies up when the bodies were ready to be released. It was mental chaos; none of them were able to think. Mike suggested that they call the funeral home that had taken care of his mother's arrangements two years before, almost to the day.

Roseann nodded. "Yes, they were very good." Marge nodded her head in agreement; she was crying again. Marge was the quiet one. She was always soft-spoken and smiling. Not a day had passed in thirty years that she had not been to her parents' house at least once, with her children in tow. Before her mom had died, she had been there several times a day. The kids were all grown now, with the last one in high school, so in addition to Marge and her daughter, her four boys were always stopping in too. This had hit them all very hard.

Roseann called and arranged a time to go to the funeral home. While they were getting ready, phones rang off the hook, both house phones and cell phones. Relatives, friends, neighbors, and media were all calling; no one seemed to be able to grasp the reality. Like the immediate family, they all wanted answers because the situation just didn't make sense. The more they watched the news, the less sense everything made. Everyone was speculating but no one really knew what had caused Diane Schuler to travel the wrong way. All anyone knew for certain was that eight people were dead.

****

Mike and his wife pulled into the funeral home parking lot. Roseann with her husband Bobby, followed, and then Marge with her husband, Joe. Joe's brother, Al Nicotina, met them there. Mike stood watching the cars on Central Avenue. To him, they looked like they were going by in slow motion. *What am I doing here?* Mike wondered.

A gentleman answered the door; Mike could tell he was at a loss for words, having heard about the accident too. The gentleman was very kind and sympathetic. Mike and his sisters tried to get the paperwork in order as the situation they were in came into focus. Mike heard it said that someone had to go to identify the bodies. His mind went blank, his body trembled, and his head spun. He didn't want to hear this, especially with his sisters sitting there. He just wanted this kind man to bring his father and brother back home to Yonkers. He would never actually know which family member went. He would never ask.

Time passed slowly, but it finally came time to choose the caskets. That brought another round of hysteria. Mike's brothers-in-law and Joe's brother would help them here. Mike stood up, and his legs started shaking. His sisters were struggling just to stand. Somehow, they all managed to get to the casket room. The director explained the choices, but the siblings just stared at him, barely hearing a word he had said. They were absorbed in their own thoughts. Finally, after what seemed like hours, a decision was made.

When the siblings and their spouses arrived back at Grandpa's house, the media crowd had grown. Mike still didn't understand why the media was there, yet in an odd way, he felt some comfort in thinking that other people cared. Cars were arriving, food was being delivered, and yet the reality that Mike had lost his father and his brother at the same time in "the accident on the news" still didn't feel real. Maybe the mind does only absorb a little at a time. The flow of people and phone calls helped occupy their minds, at least.

Once in the house, Mike and his sisters had to find papers for the funeral home—a simple task that would take what little strength they had. The funeral arrangements had to be finished. Clothes had to be chosen. The problem was the more that got done, the harder it was for Mike to hold onto the hope that it was somehow a mistake that this story on the news might not be about his family.

The local news station played the story over and over, gradually adding new video footage. It showed the cars, adding different angles; then the stretchers being wheeled in; the endless white curtain wall that, fortunately, had given the victims privacy as they were removed; and the footage of white blankets scattered around the ground. It was a hard story to even watch, and yet Mike stayed fixated. He watched it over and over again.

****

The morning following the accident, Investigator Boyle requested that New York State Police Trooper Christina Lopez notify the National Transportation Safety Board of the accident. The wrong-way crash on the Taconic Parkway was now known as the worst accident in Westchester County in 75 years. It was attracting a lot of media attention.

Investigator Shawn Hauck from Troop F Major Crimes Unit interviewed the owner of Hunter Lake Campground, Anne Scott, in Parksville, New York. This was where Diane and Daniel Schuler, along with five children, had spent the weekend. Scott stated that she had spoken with Diane on Sunday morning before Diane left. According to Scott, Diane had been in good spirits and had the five kids with her when she left. The husband had left at the same time in the truck with the dog. The Schuler's had rented a seasonal site at the campground for the past three or four years and usually came up on weekends. Ms. Scott had never had a problem with the Schuler's and they were quiet people. She'd had no report of alcohol or drug usage by them. She told Investigator Hauck, "If you need anything else let me know."

At state police headquarters in Hawthorne, New York, Investigator James Boyle conducted more interviews. The first witness stated that he had been traveling south on the Taconic at approximately 1:30 p.m. on Sunday. He had seen a minivan come to rest in the center median and had pulled over to the median. The witness had approached the vehicle and seen that the driver was still inside, along with five children, the youngest in a child seat. All of the windows except for the driver's had been closed and intact. He had seen the driver lying sideways in the vehicle. He, along with other passersby, had removed the occupants of the vehicle prior to the vehicle bursting into flames. The fire department had then arrived and taken over.

Investigator Boyle's second witness stated that he had observed the red minivan roll over down the median and that all of the windows had smashed during the roll over. He stated that he had gotten out of his car, which had been traveling on the TSP, and assisted in removing the occupants from the vehicle. He had observed the female driver being removed. He had seen three children in the third rear seat of the vehicle, including a two-year-old in a car seat on the right side. He was unable to account for the other two children.

Boyle then interviewed a witness who stated that on the day of the accident, he was driving north on the TSP in the right lane when he observed a red minivan traveling south in the northbound lanes of traffic. The witness stated that the minivan had appeared to be traveling at a high rate of speed. As soon as the vehicle had passed him, he had called 9-1-1 to report this. Boyle obtained a deposition.

The statements all told the same basic story, but differing details in the accounts showed the confusion and panic that had filled the accident scene. In listening to the witness descriptions of the scene, Boyle could determine in which order they had arrived to help. The early chaos at the scene also became evident, as the witnesses gave conflicting details of what they had seen.

Investigator Boyle took a break from the visibly shaken witnesses. He called the office in Tarrytown. New York State Police Troop T Zone Sergeant Kenneth Cano informed him that at 1:40 p.m. on the day of the accident, Jackie Hance had called the State Police Tarrytown to report a possible medical emergency with Diane Schuler. Jackie Hance had described the vehicle and advised that there were five children in the vehicle. At 1:43 p.m., Sergeant Cano had put out the description of the van over the air. At 2:12 p.m. he had called Jackie Hance back to confirm the last known location of the van and whether Diane had any known medical problems. At 2:13 p.m., he had called Diane Schuler's cell phone several times but had gone to voice mail each time.

****

At 11:00 a.m. on Monday at the New Jersey State Police Headquarters in Alpine, New Jersey, Diane Schuler's cell phone was turned in. A passerby had found the phone in a parking area adjacent to the Tappan Zee Bridge toll plaza at approximately 3:40 p.m. on the day of the accident. After calling a number from the phone, the passerby had been told that the phone may belong to someone who had been in the accident, prompting him to go to the state police. The New Jersey State Police headquarters contacted the New York State Police. Trooper John Kakavis picked up the phone and delivered it to New York State Police headquarters in Hawthorne. The calls to and from the phone were to be reviewed, pending a subpoena.

4
Signs or Suicide

July 28, 2009

The next day would not get any better. Mike and Jeanne headed back down to Yonkers early. Friends came to stay with their daughter and son. Mike and Jeanne arrived in Yonkers to be greeted by a growing media crowd and a pile of newspapers, which were all headlining the accident. Again, over coffee, the family sat together and went through the papers, hoping to get some answers. Today, the headlines had a new story: "Wrong-way driver ill before crash" and "Brother: driver in fatal wrong way crash wasn't feeling well." The story was all the same, no matter how many papers they read: Diane Schuler had called her brother, Warren Hance, two hours before driving almost two miles the wrong way on the Taconic Parkway. "During a news conference Monday, police revealed that Schuler had called her brother two hours before the crash. It's obvious something was wrong because he told her to pull over."

The police said Schuler was believed to be sober, had no known medical conditions, and wasn't taking any medications. At least six motorists had called 9-1-1. The police said they would be checking phone records to see whom Diane Schuler had called before she crashed. Neighbors of Diane Schuler stated that "she could have driven the route blindfolded"; they speculated that "something else was wrong."

The question of road signs came up. Police investigator Joseph Becerra stated, "The ramp is clearly marked with signs not to go that way, so our biggest question is, 'Why did she enter and continue traveling south in the northbound lanes.'" Locals questioned about the signs stated, "There were two *Do Not Enter* signs and *two One Way* signs." The ramp was clearly marked, but the news turned its attention to the signs. The state police were out inspecting exit ramps and interviewing witnesses, particularly the drivers who had swerved to get out of Schuler's way.

Friends and relatives were dropping by Grandpa's house, all with the same look of disbelief and sadness, and most with dark sunglasses or red eyes. Jeanne watched as Mike read through the papers. He was looking at a picture of himself on the front page, in which he was being helped up the front steps and into the house. As Mike held the paper up, Jeanne could see the back page of section B. There was a notice: "In Memoriam," with a picture of Mike's mother. Today was two years since his mom had passed on. Jeanne decided not to mention the picture now.

Mike walked out to the patio to join his brothers-in-law and nephews and a few other men gathered at the two tables. Mike's brother-in-law Bobby looked up and asked, "So, Mike, what do you think about the exit signs?"

They all looked at Mike. He was shaking his head. "You got to be kidding me. My father and brother are dead, and they're talking about signs." He continued his voice low and calm, "Why did she keep driving for two miles with people blowing the horns, flashing lights, and swerving off the road?"

"The *Daily News* claims the brother said she was sick and disoriented," Mike's nephew Danny said, pointing to the paper.

"What the hell was the brother doing for those two hours?" Mike's nephew Nicky asked. "What illness makes you drive a car the wrong way? He's obviously full of shit."

Mike's brother-in-law Joe stood up. "How the hell can you drive two miles the wrong way? How do you keep going when you have five kids in the car? How do you do that?" He was shaking his head.

A round of head nodding and mumbled agreements followed his statement. Mike sat down.

Bobby looked at Mike. "I'm hearing some talk that she might have done it intentionally," Bobby said softly, not taking his eyes off Mike.

Mike nodded. "I know; some of the reporters have mentioned suicide."

"With five kids in the car?" Joe was angry. "Unbelievable."

"Murder-suicide; it happens," Bobby said. "It's hard for me to believe, too, but it makes some pieces fit."

"If that's the case, she hit my family intentionally." Mike's voice was low. "When I watch the news, I keep thinking what the chance was that they were the car in that accident," Mike said, his voice thick and distraught.

Mike's brothers-in-law were concerned about him. They knew the pain he was in, but at the same time, they wanted him to know what was going on. He didn't need any more surprises.

"I know," Bobby added. "But the eyewitnesses are saying she was flying down the parkway, staying in her lane, and ignoring all the warnings. There is no reason she should have even been on the Taconic Parkway; it is the opposite direction from where she was heading. She would have had to travel north, then turn around and head south in the northbound lanes. It is not on the way to Long Island. It doesn't leave a whole lot of options."

Mike nodded and walked back inside. He also knew how hard it was for Bobby and Joe. His father and brother had been like a father and brother to them also. They all had a lot of years together. Mike also knew they would be looking out for him and keeping up on all the news, speculation, and rumors. *That's how it is in an Italian family,* he thought.

Outside, the conversation continued. The sign theory, that Diane Schuler had mistakenly entered the exit ramp because warning signs had not been posted appropriately to warn a normal driver, was not making sense to anyone. It was reasonable to believe a motorist could enter an exit ramp accidently, but that would not explain why Diane had kept driving for almost two miles into oncoming traffic. Other motorists had been warning her, flashing lights, blowing horns, swerving out of her way, and yet she had continued to speed toward oncoming traffic. Poor signage could not explain that bizarre behavior.

In early afternoon, Mike and his sisters had to make another trip to the funeral home. The clothing had to be dropped off along with some papers. Once they were all inside the office and seated, the funeral director gave Mike and his sisters their brother and father's personal belongings, which had been recovered from the accident, in two plastic bags. Roseann, Marge, and Mike sat and stared, tears streaming down their faces. No one moved.

Mike finally reached out and took one bag in each hand. He held the bags as tightly as he could, realizing that these were the last items that his brother and father had worn or touched. He sat and cried in disbelief. When they left, he was still holding the bags tightly, one in each hand.

5
No Medical Cause

July 29, 2009

The Wednesday after the accident was another day with more questions than answers. The news revealed that there had been "no medical link found in fatal crash." The papers stated, "Preliminary autopsy results have found no medical cause that could explain why a woman returning home from Parksville drove a minivan nearly two miles the wrong way on the Taconic State Parkway, ending in a crash that killed her and seven other people. The autopsy of Diane Schuler did not find any conditions such as a heart attack or an aneurysm; State Police are quoted as saying. The results indicate the cause of death was consistent with a traffic accident. According to authorities, Diane called her brother Warren Hance about *two hours* before the crash complaining that she was feeling sick. Investigator Joseph Becerra said witnesses have consistently told investigators that Schuler's minivan was traveling in the same lane without swerving. 'That leaves us to believe that Ms. Schuler was neither intoxicated nor asleep at the wheel.' Investigator Becerra would not say what symptoms she described to her brother, who called State Police in Tarrytown and asked them to look for her before heading to Westchester himself. He was reporting a possible medical emergency. He wanted the police to find the vehicle because something was wrong."

Jeanne and Mike drove down to Yonkers with their kids. The first wake would be the next day, and it was time for Taija and Ike to see the family, as hard as this would be. Taija was a nervous wreck at the thought of even going to Grandpa's house. The ride down was quiet and seemed longer than usual to Mike and Jeanne.

As the car pulled onto the street, Mike and Jeanne could see police cars blocking off the cul de sac and keeping the media away from the house. Mike's family was coming out to meet the car and see the kids. As Mike and Jeanne had expected, the moment their daughter stepped out of the car, she broke down, surrounded by her cousins. Jenna, her only girl cousin on Mike's side of the family, was there to hug her, and then the long line of boys. They were all upset now but comforted each other. Mike's nephews' eyes were still red and swollen from the past few days.

Ike, still young, jumped out of the car and ran into the house. They assumed that he had to actually see that his grandpa and uncle weren't there before he would believe it. He had been saying to Mike, "Dad, just bring me to Grandpa's. I can wake him up." The family all went into the house. A lot of food had been delivered, and Mike and Jeanne hoped the kids would eat something. Once inside, Taija and Ike, along with their cousins, all started to calm down.

The phones rang constantly. Relatives and friends called from all over to check on the family and to report what news they were hearing. Everyone was still in shock. No one—least of all them—could believe this had happened to their family.

There was still a lot they had to do. The women decided to take the girls out to shop for the clothes they would need for the next three days and to pick up whatever the men and boys might need. Jeanne had thought that would be easier than trying to pack that much for her family and bring it down from their house. Everyone needed something. In the early afternoon, the women and girls headed down Central Avenue to shop.

Taking the girls out proved to be a great needed relief. Sitting in the house just consumed them all in memories and sorrow. Jeanne watched Taija and Jenna choosing clothes together. Even though the girls were smiling, Jeanne could see the sadness in their eyes. *They should be shopping for vacation clothes right now,* she thought.

It was heartbreaking for Jeanne to watch as they grabbed assorted black outfits to show each other, getting each other's opinion. They had no idea how to plan for the next three days. Jeanne was startled by Marge touching her arm, "Are you okay?" Marge asked.

"Oh yeah, I was watching the girls. I feel so sorry for them," Jeanne answered.

"I know. Jenna is really a mess; this is the best I have seen her. Did you find anything to wear?" Marge asked.

"Not yet, but I will. Where's Roseann?" Jeanne asked.

"Looking at shoes," Marge said. "What do you think of this?" she asked, holding up a long black skirt.

"It's nice; buy it. I'm going to find your sister; keep an eye on the girls," Jeanne said.

****

Mike and Bob had to go back to the funeral home to take some personal items that the family wanted placed in the casket drawers. After being greeted by the funeral director, they sat in the office and discussed last-minute details. The director then told Mike that his father was ready and asked if he would like to see Mike Sr. now.

Mike looked at Bobby; neither spoke. Mike felt his heart racing and his legs tremble. "Yes, I would," he said. The director walked them back to the room, where Mike saw his father for the first time since the accident. He looked at his father with disbelief and thought about Guy coming in to join Mike Sr. He could feel his own heart pounding as if it would jump out of his chest. As shocked as he was to see his father, Mike was surprised that his dad looked so good, perfectly at peace, as if he was sleeping. For a moment, it didn't even feel real to Mike. The past few days' news of the "horrific fiery crash" didn't seem like it could have been about his father. They were alone in there, Mike and his dad, and it was quiet and peaceful. Tears streamed down Mike's face as he simply stared at his dad laying there in his suit in that big empty room. In his mind, he could separate this from the outside world and look at his father with only the thoughts he wanted to remember. He touched his father's arm, he studied his face, and he thought he could almost hear his voice...

After a while, Bob touched Mike's arm, and they quietly left.

****

At state police headquarters in Hawthorne, Investigator Boyle continued to take witness statements.

With no medical problems to explain Diane Schuler's behavior, they had to gather every witness account to piece together the day that had led to the deaths of eight people. The public wanted to know how something like this could happen, and they weren't buying the sign theory. Investigator Boyle also wanted to know just why this had happened.

Boyle interviewed a witness who stated that at approximately 1:35 p.m., she had been traveling north in the right lane of the Taconic State Parkway when she noticed a red minivan traveling south in the passing lane. The witness stated the driver had not been swerving and had appeared oblivious to the oncoming traffic. This had occurred just north of the 117 exit. The witness had not observed the collision.

The next witness Boyle interviewed was a man who had been traveling south on I-87 in Rockland County. This witness stated that he had observed a red minivan being operated by a white female in an aggressive manner. The vehicle had been straddling the right and middle lanes and cutting in and out of traffic. He stated that the driver of the minivan had had both hands on the wheel and, although cutting in and out of traffic, appeared to be doing it skillfully. He further stated that at one point, he had seen four or five children in the car. The children had not appeared to be acting unusually. He described the driver's facial expression as normal and said she had appeared to be wearing glasses, possibly sunglasses. The witness stated that he had gone through the toll booth in Harriman between 12:00 and 12:15 p.m.

This witness's story placed the erratic driving further back in the timeline than others had, but the stories were sounding mostly the same.

Another witness stated that he had been traveling northbound on the TSP in the middle lane. As he had approached the exit ramp for the Pleasantville Road exit, he had observed a red minivan coming up the ramp in the wrong direction. The van had then driven southbound in the right lane and passed him. After the vehicle had passed, he had observed in the rearview mirror as the vehicle jumped from the right lane to the left lane. He had been unable to determine if it was a male or female driver but did indicate that the driver had been wearing glasses and appeared to be focused, with their hands in the ten o'clock and two o'clock positions.

Investigator Boyle pondered the statements he had taken. *What really happened here?* He wondered.

6
First Day of the Wake

July 30, 2009

The family all gathered at Grandpa's house to get ready for the first wake service. The anxiety of seeing his father and brother laid out together was overwhelming to Mike. As the family all dressed and others arrived at the house, Mike could feel the tension that had been building slowly all morning. The quiet was unusual because the immediate family was close to thirty people. Typically, there was almost nothing but noise. Today was very noticeably different. Without talking, everyone just started walking to the cars for the drive to the funeral home.

As Mike pulled his car into the parking lot, he realized it was actually a beautiful day. He watched the rest of the family cars pull in, and all sense of beauty left him. He started shaking, and his stomach ached. As the cars unloaded, Mike's tension grew. Jeanne exited the car first and noticed cameramen from several news stations. She walked around the car to where Mike still sat. As Mike exited the car, all the cameras suddenly and simultaneously turned, focusing on him. Jeanne realized how strong a resemblance there was between Mike and his brother. It would be obvious to the news people who he was. Mike didn't notice the cameras at all.

The family gathered and waited together at the door of the funeral home. The director opened the door to greet them. That walk down the hall seemed endless. The director opened the double doors, and Mike's heart pounded and his legs went weak. He walked in, looking at the floor. When he finally looked up, he first saw his father, then, turning his head slightly, he saw his brother. Time froze; only his shaking continued. When Mike walked up to his father, his legs gave out. He landed on his knees and looked at his dad, again thinking how calm and peaceful Mike Sr. looked. He touched his dad's arm. He studied his dad's face. Myriad memories swirled through his head. The shaking started again, along with that stabbing pain in his stomach. He grabbed his father and hung on, hoping if he stayed like this, it would not be real, if he could just hold on to his father, he would not be gone. Bobby and Joe helped Mike up; he had no idea how long he had been on his knees. He didn't care. It was not supposed to have ended like this.

Mike had to move to his brother, but he couldn't. He didn't want to. He was too weak to move. His head was pounding, the smell of flowers overpowering. He felt like the room was spinning. His chest was heaving. Bobby and Joe helped him over to the second casket. He kneeled down at his brother's side. *My younger brother,* he thought. *I had always looked out for you, Guy.* The pain was taking over all his senses. It was pain too great to bear. He honestly could not believe what he was seeing. *My only brother just lying there,* he thought. So lifeless, minus the incredible smile and jovial laugh, and yet he also looked like he was just sleeping. At that moment, Mike just wanted to disappear. It seemed like it would just be easier to disappear. This *being* was too much to bear. He didn't know how long he was at his brother's side. People were helping him back to a chair. He realized that the uncontrollable sobbing he heard was coming from him. As he sat there, he watched his nephews, cousins, and friends gathering and slowly walking in.

Flowers lined the walls in both rooms. Later, Mike would look at those flowers in amazement—flowers from those he had known all of his life and even some from people he had never known. He spotted a large floral arrangement that offered sympathy from "the caring public." He was stunned. *People who never knew my dad and brother have taken the time to offer their sympathy.* He was so moved, he wept. He looked at all the pictures that had been assembled. A thousand memories clouded his mind. Happier times…the picture of his father, his brother, and himself that one of his nephew's had taken not that long ago. *The three of us, the bond that could never be broken,* Mike thought. *How could this be happening?*

Between the viewings, the family went back to Grandpa's house. Friends, relatives, and the press seemed to be everywhere. The news continued the story. It was on several channels. Calls were coming in from friends and relatives from all over the country and several other countries, everyone still wondering and speculating how such a tragedy could have happened.

That evening when the family returned to the funeral home, the media was everywhere. People lined up in hundreds. *I never thought we knew this many people,* Mike thought. He was amazed at how many people cared and had come to pay their respects to his father and brother. Their words echoed through his mind: "I'm just another prayer out there for you," and "I'm here for you." Hardly a dry eye entered. Everyone stopped to offer their sympathy, even if just a word. Watching his father's family enter made it even harder for Mike. He knew that look in their eyes; he felt that pain, and just watching them made it hurt more. *Nonstop people and nonstop agony,* Mike thought. The line seemed like it was a mile long, with some people they had not seen in years. It went on for hours. Every person who passed through touched Mike's heart. He would remember every face.

When they returned to Grandpa's house that evening, the television was already on. Mike turned around and saw his father and brothers pictures on the news. The story didn't sound or feel like it was about his family, but the faces belonged to them.

Roseanne wanted each of the grandchildren to write something down about their grandfather and uncle, a line or two, to be included in the eulogy. This would prove to be tortuous for most of them, but they were all determined. Guy had been the godfather to both of Mike and Jeanne's children, a role he had always taken seriously, and Mike Sr. was the only grandfather their daughter could really remember and their son had ever known.

Mike, Jeanne, and their children drove home that night in almost total silence. It had been a long and emotionally draining day. Once home, Mike watched as Taija tearfully wrote her contribution to the eulogy and then helped Ike write his.

Mike had decided that he wanted to write his own letter to his father and brother. This took hours. Mike would start one sentence and then break down. With Jeanne helping, it finally got done. Once he got through enough words, Jeanne could put them into a meaningful sentence. Jeanne found it incredibly sad to watch Mike struggle through, but he was determined to write his own thoughts down, no matter how hard it was. They worked on the letter well into the night. When it was finally done, it was beautiful; more importantly, it had come from his heart.

****

Another day and still no answers for anyone. Investigator Boyle asked Daniel Quinones from the state police in Liberty to go to the McDonald's in the Village of Liberty to try to obtain any video of Diane Schuler and the children in that location because Warren Hance had previously stated that Diane and the children had been planning to get breakfast on the way home.

After making his request, Boyle interviewed another witness, a volunteer firefighter who had seen the smoke from the accident and responded to the scene of the minivan. He, along with six or seven other passersby, had pulled the adult female from the vehicle and then removed the five children. He stated that all five children had been seat-belted.

Boyle then interviewed a woman who stated that she had seen the van come to rest in the median and then pulled over and removed a CPR mask from her vehicle. She had observed the adult female being removed from the vehicle first and then two of the children, one of whom was Brian, being removed from the rear of the vehicle. The other three children were removed from the side of the vehicle. She stated that some of the passersby were giving CPR to the female children. Brian was not given CPR. She confirmed that all the children had been seat-belted.

Boyle interviewed another man who stated that he had been traveling in the left lane northbound on the TSP in the area of Pace University. At approximately 1:35 p.m., the witness had observed a red minivan coming toward him. This van had been partially in the lane and partially on the shoulder. He stated that he had moved to the center lane to avoid a head-on collision. He further stated that the van had kept coming straight as if he was not even there.

Investigator Morrison took a deposition from a man who stated that he had been traveling north on the Taconic Parkway in the left lane at approximately 1:35 p.m. when he had observed a red minivan coming toward him. The van had been halfway on the shoulder and halfway in the passing lane, the witness said. He had moved his car into the center lane as the van kept coming toward him, and when he looked at the driver, she had appeared as though nothing was wrong and had just kept driving.

Boyle interviewed the next witness, who made similar statements but added that she had been a passenger in a car and had immediately dialed 9-1-1. More witnesses described the same story. Some said the van's driver had made no effort to avoid striking other vehicles and that they had not seen her brake lights go on.

These were the lucky ones who had been on the Taconic that Sunday; they must have all considered that at some point. It was the turn that had removed visibility for the oncoming traffic that ended the ride from hell.

And then a new and interesting twist turned up in the investigation. Investigator Boyle interviewed a witness who stated that on the day of the accident, while traveling from upstate New York to his home, he had turned off of I-84 at exit 4 East onto Route 17 in Orange County. Traffic had been moving well at the time. While traveling in the right lane before the Harriman toll, he had observed a red or maroon minivan pass him and start tailgating the car in front of it aggressively. This had continued for at least a minute, with the minivan alternately turning on the left blinker, and then the right, at one point riding the lane dividing line. When the car in front of the minivan had been able to move over to the right lane, it did, and the minivan had immediately moved on to start tailgating the next car in front of it. This vehicle then continued ahead. He stated that he later checked his E-Z Pass records, which indicated that he had gone through the Harriman tolls at 12:14 p.m. After going through the tolls, he had continued south on I-87. While traveling south on I-87, he had observed the same minivan pulled over to the right shoulder, and as they had approached, they had seen a woman wearing beige pants put her leg over the guardrail. The woman had lowered her head and the witness's wife had commented, "That's the same minivan from before and it looks like she's getting sick."

A similar story was given by the next witness, who stated that he had been traveling south on I-87 between noon and 12:30 p.m. when he had observed a red minivan pulled over on the right side of the road just before the Ramapo rest area. He stated in the police report:

I think I saw a white female outside the minivan. After I passed this minivan, I looked in my rearview mirror and saw the same vehicle pull back onto the thruway. Within a few minutes the same red minivan approached my car and was tailgating on my bumper. I was traveling 65 MPH and the driver of the minivan began honking repeatedly. The honking lasted about one mile. At one point the red minivan actually tried to pass me on the right shoulder but for whatever reason she pulled back into the right lane behind me. I then pulled into the rest area and the minivan followed me in. I stayed straight to take the turn for the car area the red minivan steered to the truck parking. I saw the minivan travel off the road and onto the grass and then back onto the road. The van then stopped and the female got out. I did not notice any passengers in or around the minivan, but it was hard to see inside. We did not see it when we came out.

So far, two witnesses had seen Diane Schuler stopped to vomit after leaving Liberty and before the Tappan Zee Bridge. The cell phone calls mentioned by Warren Hance would have been made around this time.

7
Second Day of the Wake

July 31, 2009

The phone rang at Grandpa's house; it was an investigator from the state police. He asked if he could stop by with some information. The family set the time for noon, knowing they had to be ready by 1:30 for the wake service. When the investigator arrived, Mike watched him walk up the steps, feeling some comfort and not knowing why. He went into his father's den with his sisters and the detective. The investigator introduced himself as James Boyle. The siblings waited. First, Inspector Boyle informed the siblings that he was going to see Carmine S., a woman who had been shown by the local news claiming to have been at the accident scene. In the broadcast, Carmine S. had been showing jewelry from the crash site on her coffee table. When the camera had zoomed in, Mike had recognized his brother's watch and ring but couldn't understand why or how this woman had the items. Investigator Boyle was also concerned about why and how Carmine S. had this jewelry, explaining to the family that it was "removing evidence from a crime scene." He did not seem happy about that. He told Mike and his sisters that he would return the jewelry to them.

Investigator Boyle also asked them to sign a permission form to retrieve the black box from their brother's car, which Roseanne did. The black box was part of the air bag system on Guy's late-model car and would give the police information about the seconds just prior to the crash, such as the vehicle's last recorded speed and the braking, accelerating, and other data from the vehicle.

Then came the bombshell. Investigator Boyle told Mike and his sisters that the toxicology reports were back and showed that Diane Schuler had been blasted drunk and high at the time of the crash. She'd had a blood alcohol content of 0.19, more than twice the legal limit, and even higher readings of THC, the active ingredient in marijuana. For that instant, it was as if the world stood still. No one moved or made a sound. Mike looked at the investigator, dumbfounded. The detective stared at him.

Investigator Boyle continued, he had told them about the alcohol out of respect for the family so they would not be blindsided by the media. They were very grateful for that. Boyle asked them not to release this information because the media would not get the news until after all the victims' funerals.

Boyle assured Mike Sr.'s children and their families that the police would be investigating this thoroughly, long after there was snow on the ground, he said. The police, too, wanted to know what had happened and who may have contributed to the accident. Investigator Boyle also told them that Daniel Schuler and the Hance family were not cooperating as much as the police would have liked. Suspicions had started growing in the official investigation and within Mike's family.

Mike suspected then that they were in for disaster. He was crying again and hugged Detective Boyle. At least now, he had something that made sense. *Diane Schuler was drunk.* Mike's head was throbbing. *My family was killed by a drunk. A drunken mother killed her own child and three nieces.* The news had hit him like a bullet. Thoughts of the past few days swirled through Mike's mind. He tried to organize his thoughts. He looked at his two sisters—they just sat and cried. He called his wife, Bobby, and Joe into the room and told them the news and explained that it should not leak out. The spouses were all as shocked as the siblings—after all, the police had made statements saying that they'd had no reason to suspect alcohol. Everyone had basically ruled it out. The suicide theory had made more sense. It had been consistent with witness accounts. This was worse. It was impossible to believe that not one person Diane Schuler encountered that day would not have known this. Once again, a room in Grandpa's house was full of tears and anger. Would it ever end?

The adults composed themselves and got ready for the second wake service. They did not want the kids to know this information yet. It would be too hard for them to keep quiet and too painful to hear.

Mike could not stop thinking about how Diane Schuler could have done this. It just did not make sense. He had heard that she had left the campground early that Sunday morning and had been with her husband. The questions kept going through his mind: *How did her husband not know anything about his wife leaving that way and what went on in that car? It doesn't make any sense. A woman with that much alcohol in her system and that much marijuana in her system leaves a campground with five children and he leaves with a dog?* He wanted answers to all these questions.

That day, speculation was growing, especially within the media. No one had answers, and nothing added up. How could this woman drive two miles the wrong way on the Taconic? The family found that *knowing* began to make coping with the loss that much harder. *Drunk and high* kept running through Mike's head. What had been unbearable pain before was now mixed with unbelievable anger.

The family arrived at the afternoon wake, Mike, his sisters and their spouses feeling uneasy from the new information. It was a lot to absorb and to keep inside while droves of people came and went, all paying their respects—all distraught and wanting answers...the answers the family now knew but couldn't share. The family had been told that releasing the information could compromise the investigation. Not wanting to do that, they kept the information quiet.

When the family returned to the house again between services, the phone just rang and rang. The news channels and newspapers called for updates, comments, and news. They offered headlines but no answers. It was becoming obvious to everyone involved—the family and their friends, the police, and especially the media—that there was more to this story than met the eye. The news played the story over and over with pictures of the victims and pictures of the crash site. It was surreal. In response to the growing media presence, the Yonkers Police had stationed more officers in the area and had come to block off the street and keep the media away from the house. The family suspected that the Yonkers Police had also been told of the toxicology findings. It was comforting to see them and just know they were there.

More people were at the house now, and the food had already been delivered and set up. Mike showed Jeanne that a button had come off his jacket. She suggested that he wear a different jacket. "No, I really wanted to wear this" Mike answered, looking upset. Jeanne said she would sew the button back on. When Mike said, "I can't find the button," Jeanne realized that the issue was not about the button.

Roseann's son Richie and his girlfriend Rian were standing near them. "I can drive you to my tailor, Jeanne," Rian volunteered. "I'm sure he can fix it while we wait."

"Are you sure, Rian? That is a lot to ask," Jeanne said.

"Yes, come on" Rian answered.

Within forty minutes the women were back with the jacket repaired. Mike seemed grateful.

"Thank you, Rian. Mike is just frazzled. Normally, he doesn't care what he wears," Jeanne said.

"I know that. I'm happy to help," Rian said.

The family returned to the funeral home for the final night. It seemed more crowded than the night before. The mayor of Yonkers came to pay his respects. Mike was impressed. The mayor seemed sincere as he handed Mike his card and told him to call if he needed anything. Jeanne was pretty certain that everyone knew there was more to this story. The captain of the fire department that had been on the scene also came to pay his respects. Mike felt an almost instant connection; this man had been there with Mike's family and knew more about what had happened that day than Mike did. The American Legion also came that evening. They had a beautiful prayer and honor service for Mike's father under the direction of Mike Jr.'s cousin Pete. Pete and Mike Sr. had been close and Pete was taking this very hard.

Facing the family and the crowd of mourners was as hard now knowing the truth as it had been earlier in the afternoon. Roseann and Marge looked totally drained. One by one, the family members were falling apart. It was hard for them to look at Mike Sr. and Guy and know that they had died at the hands of a drunk. It should never have happened. Mike's family wondered what the other family was going through. To bury all of your children was beyond the unthinkable. Jeanne glanced at her daughter and thought about the three little sisters. Jeanne had seen the girls' pictures on the news for days and had pictured her own daughter at those ages. Her heart ached for the woman she didn't know. How, she wondered, would the investigators tell that poor woman that someone she trusted had been drunk and had killed her girls? Jeanne tried to block the thoughts from her mind, but still, those girls were a part of this nightmare. She imagined the feeling she was experiencing was the same for all of Mike's family. Fortunately, the crowds of mourners helped to ease her pain;

they occupied her mind, and knowing that people care offered her great comfort.

Mike, Jeanne, and their kids were staying in Yonkers that night because the funeral was the next morning. Jeanne, gazing around Grandpa's living room, saw that everyone looked extremely stressed and tired. They were all running on adrenaline. Mike decided to sleep in his brother's room that night. As he lay there, Mike could feel the hurt starting to take over his body. He began to grasp the reality that his brother really wasn't here anymore, that his father was not here anymore—the horror of knowing that they were really gone. *This was his brother's room, and Mike should not be there*, he thought. Mike did not sleep that night.

Upstairs, Roseann and Marge were still working on the eulogy. Their friend since childhood, Inez, who had immediately flown up from Florida, was helping, while Jeanne typed out what they completed. It had already been a long night, and it was about to get a lot longer. They had learned too much to absorb for one day, and no one had really slept in days. They were simply going through the motions and helping each other. It was even harder, they were sure, because they were also watching everything on the news and everyone had an opinion about what had happened and could see the horror that their loved ones had suffered.

Sitting at the kitchen table, the women kept their conversation quiet. Roseann and Marge were struggling with the news from the investigator. Roseann looked at Jeanne. "I told Inez about the accident."

Jeanne nodded and said, "Everyone will know soon. It bothers me more about the jewelry."

"Why?" Inez asked.

"I don't believe Guy's ring and watch just fell off and landed in the same place for someone to find." Jeanne answered.

Inez looked at Jeanne and nodded her head, "wait and see what the investigator finds out," Inez answered.

Jeanne just nodded.

****

On the morning of July 31, Investigators Quinones and Young arrived at the McDonald's in Liberty, New York, at approximately 11:30 a.m. and reviewed the video for July 26. They observed Diane Schuler and the five children enter the McDonald's at 9:56 a.m. and then leave at 10:33 a.m. Footage showed Diane Schuler ordering food and the children later playing in the play area. McDonald's employees were not able to burn a DVD of the incident while Investigators Young and Quinones were there. (The DVD was eventually received and reviewed by Investigator Boyle on August 8, 2009.)

At approximately 10:00 a.m., Investigators Boyle and Becerra arrived at the Westchester County Medical Center in Valhalla and met with Daniel Schuler. They interviewed Mr. Schuler regarding the weekend of July 25 and 26 and his camping trip with his family. Mr. Schuler stated that he had driven his Toyota Tundra to the campground on Thursday with his dog. His wife and kids, along with their nieces, had arrived on Friday. He said that on Friday evening after dinner, he had drank a couple of beers and his wife had had two strawberry daiquiris. He stated that on Saturday, he and his wife had taken the kids to a combination amusement and water park nearby. He said that on Saturday evening they had stayed at the campsite and that neither he nor his wife had drank that evening. The children had gone to bed at about 9:00 p.m. and he and his wife had gone to sleep at 11:30 p.m. Mr. Schuler stated that he had awakened at approximately 5:00 a.m. on Sunday and the rest of the family had got up around 8:00 a.m. He stated that he and his family had left the campsite between 9:00 and 10:00 a.m.—he in his truck with the dog and she in her brother's van with the kids. Daniel stated that his wife had been going to take the kids to McDonald's in Monticello for breakfast. He stated that he and his wife usually took the same route home to Long Island, which was Route 17 to I-87 to I-287 to I-95 to the Throgs Neck Bridge. He said he had not spoken to his wife on his way home and had received a call from his brother-in-law, Warren Hance, stating that Diane had been in an accident with the kids. Mr. Schuler stated that his wife had no medical issues and was in good health. He stated that she did not have a primary care physician or abuse any type of medications. Mr. Schuler stated that his wife drank very little alcohol.

Boyle then advised Mr. Schuler of the preliminary toxicology results regarding the presence of alcohol and marijuana, to which Mr. Schuler replied that he had not seen his wife drink on Sunday but that she smoked marijuana once in a while to relieve the stress of work and the kids. He added that she was in charge of credit and collections at Cablevision. Mr. Schuler told Investigator Boyle that he was employed by the Nassau County Police Department as a security guard and worked the 4:00 p.m. to midnight shift. He stated that he and his wife had been together for 13 years and had been married six or seven years, he didn't remember exactly. They had been going camping for approximately 11 years.

After meeting with the Bastardi family around noon and telling them about the results of the tox report, Investigator Boyle, accompanied by Investigator Gary Bedel, arrived in Long Island to interview Warren and Jackie Hance. They were met at the door by an off-duty NYPD Detective DiCarlo. Boyle asked DiCarlo if he might speak to Warren and Jackie Hance. DiCarlo stated that Warren was on his way to the Westchester County Medical Center to visit Brian Schuler.

Boyle called Investigator Becerra to advise him of Warren's destination. Becerra, wanting to give all the family members information about the tox report on the same day, said he would meet Warren Hance at the hospital. Boyle asked DiCarlo if he could briefly speak to Jackie Hance. DiCarlo advised him that Jackie did not wish to speak to the police. Boyle then advised DiCarlo that he did not intend to ask her any questions but wanted to provide her with some information. DiCarlo then entered the house. When he returned, he stated that Jackie did not want to see them.

At 3:30 p.m., Investigator Becerra and Investigator Morrison arrived at Westchester County Medical Center and interviewed Warren Hance and Joan (Jay) Schuler (sister-in-law of Daniel Schuler). Mr. Hance stated that on the day of the accident, he had received a call from his daughter Emma sometime in the morning while he was at his office, a few blocks from his home. Emma had told him that they were on their way home from the campground and should be home at about 1:00 p.m. Mr. Hance stated that everything had seemed fine. Shortly after, he said, he had received another call from Emma stating that they would be home closer to 1:30 p.m. Twenty minutes later, Mr. Hance had arrived home and his wife, Jackie, had told him that she had just got off the phone with Diane Schuler and that something was wrong with Diane. Jackie had also told Warren that the kids were crying in the background. Mr. Hance said he had called his sister, who appeared to be having problems communicating. She had seemed to be disoriented, had problems talking, and had called her brother, "Danny". Mr. Hance said his sister hadn't been herself on the phone and that he had her put Emma on the phone. Emma had told him they were okay and that they were stopped. When Mr. Hance had asked his daughter if she could see any road signs, Emma had said there were signs that said Sleepy Hollow and Tarrytown. Mr. Hance said he had told {them} to stay where they were and he was coming to get them. Mr. Hance stated that he had his wife contact the Tarrytown and Sleepy Hollow Police and then had gone to get his father, who lived nearby and who could drive one of the cars back. Mr. Hance and his father had stopped at the state police office in Tarrytown and asked the troopers to look for Diane and the kids, describing the vehicle and explaining that there may be some type of problem or medical condition. He stated that he also asked for an Amber Alert on the vehicle. Mr. Hance told Investigator Becerra that he and his father continued driving around, looking for Diane and the kids. He stated that he called his sister's cell phone continually from the time he left his home in Long Island and stated that he had eventually gone back to the state police in Tarrytown and had been met by two troopers who told him to go to Westchester County Medical Center. Mr. Hance said that his sister drank only socially and would normally drink pina coladas and daiquiris. He told Investigator Becerra that this was the first time this season that his kids had gone camping with his sister and brother-in-law and that they had gone once the previous year. He also stated that this was the first year Diane and Daniel had stayed at this particular campground and that in years past they had camped in the Adirondacks.

Jay Schuler told Investigator Becerra that Diane smoked marijuana regularly. She stated that Diane didn't believe in medicine and used marijuana to relax. Diane usually smoked at night after the kids went to bed, Jay said. Both Warren Hance and Joan Schuler stated that Diane was in excellent health and had no medical conditions.

8
The Funeral

August 1, 2009

Mike awoke in the morning, dreading the funeral. The whole family did. There's something about knowing it's the last day, the last viewing that fills you with overwhelming sadness. Few are prepared for this last and final good-bye. A sense of total panic overcomes you. The family all moved around silently inside the house getting ready for the funeral. A large pot of coffee was set up in the kitchen. No one had slept much, but no one felt tired. Mike looked around at his nephews all dressed in black suits and trying not to show the agony they felt. Three of their girlfriends, Rian, Kristy, and Jess, tried to force smiles when they saw Mike—beautiful girls whose faces now showed days of tearstains. His nephew Joey had arrived with his wife, Christina, and their two young children. Any other day, their little girl would look as if she were going to a party all dressed up, but today there was no smile on her face. Joey and Christina's son Joe-Joe had always been quiet; Mike noticed today that he kept his head down, avoiding all eye contact. Mike looked at his daughter and his niece Jenna; they were at the table moving donuts around their plates without any bites missing. It was an overwhelming sight to see these kids today, Mike thought.

The police were already at the house waiting to escort the family. The lights were already on waiting for the limos. The family all walked to the waiting cars in silence. Perhaps everyone was afraid that the wrong word would set the whole family off. As the cars approached the funeral home, police on motorcycles were also arriving. The funeral home had done a good job in keeping everything private.

Mike couldn't get past knowing that he would not see his father and brother again even if in a funeral home. This would be the final walk-by, the moment he knew must finally end. He watched his family breakdown, one by one. He watched the agony and the tired faces. It was hard to remember happiness.

Mike walked up to see his brother. He put his arms around Guy and held on, set his head on Guy's chest, unable to let him go. He told Guy that he would get answers and that he would get justice for Guy and their dad. Mike was helped up from the kneeler at the casket and went to see his dad for the last time. He put his hands on his dad's face and told him that he would not give up. After almost collapsing, Mike was helped from the casket and was taken outside.

They all walked to the waiting limos. Policemen lined up to get them to the church. Mike sat in the limo and waited for the hearse to take the front. He knew his brother-in-law Joe would wait inside and watch the caskets get closed. Mike also knew how hard that would be for Joe, and he felt immense gratitude and relief to have Joe as his brother-in-law. He had learned over the years that Joe was someone he could depend on. Joe's brother, Al, was the same way. At the funeral mass, Al Nicotina would be reading the letter that Mike had written for his father and brother. Mike knew he could trust Al for that, as hard as it would be for Al.

Looking around, Mike saw cars waiting and onlookers passing. The ride to the church brought total silence. The police escort surrounded them. It was an impressive sight Mike thought—nine policemen on motorcycles. He could not help but feel really good for the moment. The police represented four precincts from the area and the New York State Police. They lined up in perfect formation and moved about with skill and confidence like a well-practiced military drill. At each cross street the two policemen at the rear raced up alongside the long line of cars and took the lead. The lead two closed the next set of streets and stopped traffic. In spite of the despair surrounding the family, they found the coordination of the police escort magnificent to see and a wonderful tribute to Guy and Mike Sr. Mike was ecstatic that this was for his father and brother. It gave a sense of importance to the funerals for the family he would bury that day. It brought back the dignity and privacy for his loved ones that had been lost with all the news coverage. These weren't just victims of the Taconic Tragedy; they were his father and brother, and they were important.

For the first time in days Mike experienced a feeling of warmth. He made a mental note to thank everyone. He wasn't even sure whom to thank but he thought that the mayor must have arranged this. He was proud to be back in Yonkers—here where his parents had moved from the Bronx to give them a better life. Now, Yonkers had come together to let his dad know that it had been the right choice. *People care, and they let us know*, Mike thought.

At the church the family was received by four priests. Dozens of reporters and cameras lined the street across from the church. The family left the cars to wait for the caskets to be removed and carried into the church. Standing on the church steps Mike realized for the first time that it was another beautiful day. He looked around at the huge crowd now assembled. He could have heard a pin drop as the caskets were removed from the car.

Mike's nephews, Inez's son Justin, and a few assigned gentlemen served as pallbearers. Mike's daughter and niece followed them. They looked sad and yet determined at the same time. Watching the kids was painful. Each face twisted into the agony of grief. Mike's young son Isaiah, grabbed on to walk with the casket. It had not been that long ago that Isaiah had been baptized here, Mike thought, with Guy as his godfather. He pictured his brother walking Ike down that same aisle. *And now there is my son walking my brother down.* Mike's heart ached.

The immediate family followed the procession. It was the longest walk Mike could remember. He was shocked to see how many people were in the church. Once seated, he glanced at his family. His daughter caught his eye. *I don't know how I can help her get through this*, he thought. The look on Taija's face made him wonder if life could ever be the same as it had been. She was devastated and his son was too young to even understand how things like this could happen.

When the service started, Mike hoped it would never end. He didn't notice the slew of reporters in the balcony area. The service included the eulogy, the full mass, and the reading of the letters the kids had all written, each one sadder than the next. Then Al and his wife, Sally, read what Mike had written. Mike listened intently as Al began to read. When Al was overcome by emotion, Sally finished the reading. Mike was both relieved and appreciative. He felt satisfied with what he had written, the final words to his father and brother.

Following the procession out was worse than following it into the church because the final good-byes and the final tribute were over. It left only the trip to the final resting place. The flower car, two hearses, four limousines, and scores of cars were about to take Mike's father and brother for the last drive by their home, the house in which they had shared a million memories and a thousand holidays. As the procession approached the street, the police stopped all traffic and held the procession back. Only the first seven cars would do the drive-by. Jeanne looked at Mike and saw that he had his head down and was rubbing his hands together. She wondered how he would get through this.

The ride to the cemetery seemed to go too quickly. Mike looked out the back window of the limo and realized there was an endless line of cars. The police had stopped traffic on the Sprain Parkway to allow the procession. He couldn't see the end of the line of cars, it was that long.

They arrived at the cemetery and waited in the cars for all the others to park and walk the long distance before proceeding to the gravesite. Mike stood dazed during the graveside service and the twenty-one–gun salute for his dad. It was a beautiful service. From the corner of his eye Mike saw Isaiah run out and pick something up, putting it in his pocket. Not ready to leave right after the service, Mike waited to watch the caskets get lowered. He had to see it through no matter how hard it was. As they were leaving Ike walked over to him and handed Mike one of the shells from the military gun salute. With tears in his eyes Ike said, "Here, Dad, this is for you." Mike took the shell; with tears in his eyes, he put it in his pocket knowing he would always keep that casing.

Mike's cousin Pete had also seen Ike pick up the shell. To Ike's surprise, Pete walked over and gave Ike another shell.

The funeral director announced the invitation to all the mourners to join the family for lunch at Mike Sr.'s house. Christina's mother Patti had arranged for catering. She was so thoughtful and organized that when the family arrived back at the house everything was set up, supplied, and ready to go. When Mike arrived back at the house, he looked around smiling to himself as he thought, *my father would say "from soup to nuts."*

9

One Week Later

August 2, 2009

It had been exactly one week since the accident. Tired, drained, and heartbroken, the entire family was still recovering from the effects of the funeral. Waking up and realizing that they had actually seen their family members for the last time was devastatingly final. They were supposed to get on with their lives but the past week had ended life the way they knew it. They found great comfort in all of them being together at Grandpa's house. The house was like a shelter from the outside world—the family did not have to face the realities of what had happened. The house had become their safe place.

The Sunday newspaper relived the funeral. The pictures showed some of the family what they had actually missed. The adults felt sad, looking at the pictures of the kids that the paper had printed—the pictures of children watching the caskets of their grandfather and uncle. They had been through a lot this past week.

The family was leaving the house in groups that day to attend Dan Longo's wake service. Mike drove there with his brother-in-law Bobby. After the long week they had spent at Grandpa's house and at the funeral home for Guy and Mike Sr., they were walking into yet another funeral home. After paying their respects to Dan, Mike asked to speak to Dan's brother, Joe Longo privately.

They went into another room and Mike asked Joe if he had been informed that Diane Schuler had been drunk and high. Joe had not heard, so Mike shared with him the information they had been given by Investigator Boyle. Mike let him know the information would be coming out in the news. Joseph Longo looked at him and said, "Now I'm angry. Now I am getting mad." Mike knew that feeling. He had felt the same.

They said their good-byes and Mike left. On the way home Mike and Bob discussed what had just happened. It had been hard for Mike to be the one to tell Joe Longo that a drunk driver had done this, while standing at his brother's wake. *It would be worse if he heard it first on the news*, Mike thought.

Mike's cell phone rang. The display indicated that the number was unknown. Mike answered and was a little stunned to hear the assistant district attorney of Westchester County, Jonathan Strongin on the other end of the line. He grabbed Bobby's hand and pointed to the phone. The ADA was offering condolences and assuring Mike that the office was doing everything in its power to investigate this horrific accident. Mike and the ADA spoke briefly about the drinking and pot. The ADA recapped the investigation and set up a meeting for Mike and his family with the district attorney for Wednesday. After hanging up the phone Mike looked at Bobby and asked him what he thought that had been all about. It had been a long and confusing week. He was still reeling from the shock. He didn't quite understand why this meeting was set up. He called Irving Anolik and told Irving about the call. Irving was not surprised; he explained that the accident had been ruled a homicide and that is where the DA comes in. Irving and Mike arranged to meet before Wednesday's meeting.

Mike and Bob arrived back at the house and informed the rest of the family of the upcoming meeting with the DA. Mike's family all wondered what to make of this development. Of course they had no idea what was in store for them in the days ahead. They had just gotten through a double funeral, after all.

Jeanne went to Dan Longo's service later. When she arrived a reporter and crew from a local news channel were waiting outside, the newsperson telling people that the county was out checking the exit signs and asking if they thought poor signage was a contributing factor to the accident.

Driving the wrong way at high speed, facing oncoming traffic for almost two miles? How and why anyone would try to blame the signs? Jeanne thought.

10
Last Victim's Funeral

August 3, 2009

Daniel Longo was buried. "The last of the victims' funerals" the newspapers said. But he was much more than the last of the victims. Daniel was leaving his only son behind. He was leaving behind his brother, nephews, many friends and relatives, and all the men at the veterans' hospital where he had volunteered for years—the many whose lives he touched. All gone in a flash at the hands of a drunken woman.

On this same day, a newspaper titled an article "Why Mom Drove the Wrong Way is Still a Mystery." The article stated, "Diane Schuler was a devoted mother, admired for her competence, ease with children and sense of humor. Never, *her family said*, had there been a more responsible and trusted caregiver" (emphasis added).

A drunken woman was being called the perfect and responsible mother, totally dedicated to her children. That responsible and trusted caregiver had just killed seven innocent people including four children.

It was infuriating for Mike's family to hear these remarks. What they didn't understand was why her family wasn't humiliated and embarrassed to say these things. Diane Schuler had just murdered four children...four children whom she had taken on a four-hour death ride. It was more interesting however, that no one in the family had come forward to the police about her alcohol and drug use.

****

The state police continued to piece together the accident. Investigator James Boyle was back in the office taking statements.

According to the police report, a new witness stated that "on 7/26/09 at approximately 1:30 p.m. he was traveling north in the left lane of the Taconic State Parkway. He stated that a red minivan was traveling south in the northbound passing lane, heading right towards him. The witness stated that he quickly veered into the center lane and watched through his rear view mirror, as the minivan struck the vehicle behind him. He was driving a black GMC."

Another witness stated that on July 26, he had been traveling north in the center lane of the Taconic when he saw a red minivan traveling south in the passing lane. This van was partially in the lane and partially on the shoulder. He further stated that the Trailblazer was traveling in the left lane approximately twelve feet in front of him. The witness stated that the minivan then struck the Trailblazer head-on in the passing lane and he then sped up to avoid the accident. He didn't see the third car, the Tracker get hit. His wife concurred with his statements.

It seemed that even with more eyewitness statements, the story was staying the same.

11
The News Release

August 4, 2009

Mike and Jeanne were at home and Jeanne was looking at the front page newspaper picture of Joe Longo hugging Dan's son at the funeral. Mike put the television on; the accident was all over the news. Across the bottom of the TV came the breaking-news: **Diane Schuler Drunk and High**. The accident had officially been ruled a homicide. This was the day the devil showed a face.

Within minutes, Mike's phone was ringing off the hook. The media was anxious to speak to him. They all wanted to know how he felt and how the family was taking this news. His stomach was in a knot. He kept watching the news and each time the results were announced he wondered how Diane Schuler's family could not have known she was drunk and high and why they had not stopped her. His head was aching, and that empty feeling starting in his stomach was taking over his whole body.

The family had been told the news would break on Wednesday, and they knew the results, but seeing it on the news and knowing that the public knew made it much harder to hear. *My family died at the hands of a drunk driver,* Mike thought. It just sounded too simple and preventable to have happened. Why had her brother not called 9-1-1 immediately? Why was Daniel Schuler not cooperating with the police? After all, he had been with her at the campground that morning. He was the last one to see her. He had to know her demeanor that day. With that quantity of marijuana in her system, it didn't seem possible that he would not have known about the condition she was in before she left with his children and nieces. He had had a conversation with her that morning.

The more Mike watched the news and the more phone calls came, the more doubts grew in him that no one had known Diane Schuler was drunk that day. Seven innocent people were dead and buried. He wondered if other people would be charged. These were issues he needed answers to. *My family was murdered. I have to know everything,* he thought. *How does any mother or any person, load a car with children and intentionally drink and get high? Why didn't her family stop her?*

Mike was not the only one watching the news that day. Investigator James Boyle received a phone call as news of the toxicology report was breaking. The caller was a witness who had decided to call when the press announced that alcohol had played a role in the accident. According to a police report the witness "is confident this is the woman based on a photo released." Also according to the report this witness stated "We were coming from our summer home traveling eastbound on Route 17 where the highway goes from two lanes to one(Pine Bush exit) at approximately 11:45 a.m., when I noticed a red minivan parked on the shoulder of the highway eastbound. Due to the slow traffic I noticed a middle aged white female with brown hair standing in front of the minivan bent over with her hands on her knees. The woman was facing the minivan and slightly turned towards the road. When I first saw her I thought she was coming out of the woods or something, as I got closer to her the woman was motionless in the bent over position as if she was sick or going to vomit. The woman stayed in that position after I drove past. I did not see any passengers in the van. I dozed off and about five minutes later my husband who was driving, woke me and commented about the red minivan coming up from behind in the left lane at a high rate of speed. My husband moved over to the right lane to let the red minivan pass and we both noticed it was the woman in the red minivan that we passed at exit 119 in Pine Bush, parked on the shoulder. After the minivan passed us I watched it speed by weaving in and out of both lanes passing other eastbound motorists."

Diane Schuler had left McDonald's at 10:33 a.m. and walked out of Sunoco at 10:49 a.m. according to the surveillance video. It was reported that she had seemed fine. At the Pine Bush exit in Orange County, approximately half an hour from the McDonald's and Sunoco however, she was already stopping on the side of the road to vomit with a van full of children.

Investigator Boyle received the official written toxicology report from the Westchester County laboratory and asked Investigator Randall McGregor to check liquor stores to see if anyone recalled Diane Schuler purchasing liquor that weekend. McGregor checked three liquor stores in Liberty and several in Monticello, all with negative results.

Upstate in Sullivan County, where the campground is located, Investigator Morrison took a deposition from a woman who had also been at the campground that weekend. In the deposition, the woman states, "I arrived at Hunter Lake Campground on 7/25/09 at approximately 11:30 a.m. I saw Mr. Schuler and his son Brian on their campground, said Hello, had a brief conversation about how the children were getting big, the weather, etc. I did not see Mrs. Schuler. The next time I saw Mr. Schuler he was leaving the campground around 6 or 7 a.m. on Sunday. We did not speak at that time. Later that morning I went into town at around 10:30 and returned at 1 or 2: 00 p.m. I noticed that the Schuler's' pop up was closed up and there was no one on the campsite. I assumed the family had gone home. I did not see Mrs. Schuler at all during the weekend."

12

The Headlines

August 5, 2009

The press went wild! The headlines and facts released that day stunned people near and far.

WRONG-WAY CRASH MOM DRUNK, STONED
HOW COULD SHE? (New York Post)

Diane Schuler was totally drunk and high on pot
When she caused the crashed that killed her daughter,
her nieces,
And three innocent men
HOW COULD SHE? (NY DAILY NEWS)

DRUNK AND HIGH
Police: wrong-way crash mom was intoxicated
(TIMES HERALD RECORD)

DRIVER DRUNK, HIGH, POLICE SAY

Cops: Mom smoked Pot, had 0.19% alcohol level

In crash that killed 8 (THE JOURNAL NEWS)

POLICE: MOM IN WRONG-WAY CRASH WAS DRUNK, HIGH (THE POUGHKEEPSIE JOUNAL)

Diane Schuler had a blood alcohol level of 0.19 and in addition, as much as six grams of undigested alcohol in her stomach. She had high levels of THC (113 nanograms) the chemical found in marijuana, indicating that she had smoked pot within an hour of or as recently as fifteen minutes before the crash—all while driving around for four hours in a minivan full of children and calling her brother several times from her cell phone.

The *NY Daily News* reported "'At this point we are getting limited information from the family,' said Major William Carey of the State Police. The police had found a broken 1.75 liter bottle of Absolut Vodka inside the van."

The *NY Post* reported that the chief toxicologist with the Westchester County Medical Examiner said "With the alcohol alone Schuler would have had difficulty with perception and memory. Around that level you also get tunnel vision. When combined with marijuana, those effects are intensified."

The family had arranged to meet at Grandpa's house to go to the meeting with the DA in White Plains. The DA's office would be going over what information they had gathered so far. As Mike's family was driving, they received a call from the district attorney's office. Because of the breaking news a large crowd of reporters had already gathered outside of the building, so the family was given directions to an underground parking garage where they would be met by a detective to escort them upstairs.

The group entered the garage through a security gate across the street from the herds of reporters and cameras. They were taken through back doors and hallways escorted by detectives. Arriving at the office, they were greeted with what seemed like genuine compassion. Meeting them there was the Longo family with their attorney, District Attorney Janet Difiore, Assistant DA Jonathan Strongin, Investigators Boyle and Becerra, representatives from Victim Assistance, Irving Anolik as the Bastardis' attorney, attorney Marianne Luciano from the DA's office, DA spokesman Lucien Chalfen, and several others. The introductions moved so quickly that the Bastardis' had difficulty remembering the names of everyone there.

Ms. Difiore first led Mike into another room where the windows faced the street, to show him the scores of reporters from the window. He was still dumbfounded at the media attention and numb from the pain. Ms. Difiore looked at Mike and pointed to the street. She said, "They are there for you. The public wants answers too."

The family members sat a long table and listened to the information that was available thus far. It was still an ongoing investigation, so more was still coming out. They discussed who was cooperating, who was not, who might have known Diane Schuler was drunk, who had let her drive like that.—the questions they still wanted answers to. The family members could see by the looks on the investigators' faces that they wanted the answers as much as everyone else did. This event had hit Westchester County hard. People knew any car could have been hit on the Taconic that day; this woman had made death inevitable. They had to answer the questions that the public wanted answered: Who does this to children?

At this point in the investigation, investigators had not accounted for the entire timeline of Diane Schuler's deadly trip home. It was also revealed that the Schuler's' camper had not been searched. The owner of the campground Anne Scott, had not allowed the state police access without a search warrant. Shortly after Scott had kept investigators from the camper, it had been towed to the Schulers' home and gone through by their private detective.

The investigators said that in trying to interview the Schuler and Hance families, no one had been forthcoming, most had refused to be interviewed, and the investigators had no access to Jackie Hance. Jackie was heavily medicated. There was also a suicide concern about her. The DA's office revealed to the victims' families that both Daniel Schuler and Warren Hance had hired attorneys on the day the toxicology report was released. Before this meeting, the district attorney had not been made aware that Diane Schuler had been driving Warren Hance's minivan that fateful day.

Irving Anolik asked if the DA had considered or would consider a grand jury. A grand jury would give them the right to subpoena, and because very few members of Diane Schuler's family were cooperating and, now that they had attorneys, would cooperate even less, Anolik saw the need. The DA was not considering a grand jury that day but was open to the possibility.

This meeting made the victims' families aware that the purpose of the investigation was to determine if anyone *in addition to Diane Schuler* was in any way responsible for the accident. They were investigating these things while considering her drinking, the marijuana, and the cell phone calls. If Diane Schuler's husband, Daniel, had been aware that she had been drinking, or had left the campground while knowing she was drinking, he would face charges. Had Diane still been drunk from the night before? They wanted to know if Daniel had been aware that his wife had been smoking pot, where she had gotten it, and where she had been smoking it. Investigators were also trying to figure out whom Diane had spoken to on her cell phone, what those people had known, and if they had been neglectful in not notifying the police that children were in danger. The campground claims to have a "no intoxication" policy and, of course, a "no drug" policy, but that still left questions. Were there witnesses to Diane and her husband drinking or smoking pot? Was it routine for them? Had anyone been aware that Diane had left drinking?

This event was no longer being investigated as an accident; now it was a homicide, a preventable murder.

The Bastardi family left the meeting feeling hopeful that the investigation would bring some answers. They had been told that there would be another meeting when more information was available. The Bastardis' left the DA meeting aware that there had been four cell phone calls but what had transpired after those calls was unclear. The only phone bill the police could obtain by subpoena was Diane Schuler's. They had no way of knowing if there were calls between the Hances and other Schuler family members.

Following the meeting, the attorneys spoke to the press that had gathered outside. The families meanwhile, slipped out quietly. Irving Anolik stated for the press that "Any person that knew she was drinking is an accomplice. She just didn't wake up one morning with a drug problem and capable of drinking that much alcohol. If the driver was alive, the charges would have been second-degree murder. I believe there is a strong fragrance of criminality."

Back at Grandpa's house the topic of discussion among the Bastardis' naturally, was what the families had just heard at the meeting. It was really just an abundance of more questions. They were all overwhelmed and disappointed. They had learned that neither the Hance nor Schuler family was really cooperating. This reinforced the many stories and rumors they had been hearing all week...if they *were* stories and rumors. The rumors such as Diane Schuler had found out that her husband was having an affair and that they were having marital problems and she had been drinking and smoking pot all weekend at the campsite and they had been arguing. That Jackie Hance had asked for a divorce the day after the accident. Now the rumors were starting to make some sense.

The women went to the kitchen to make coffee and the men went out to the patio. It was a hot day and the constant stress was tiring. The men were met by the older boys, who had been waiting at the house. The boys listened eagerly and they wanted immediate results, which were not going to come. This tragedy had rocked their world. July 26 was the day the impossible had become possible, the day they had become the people who "these things don't happen to."

Bob lit a cigarette and looked at Mike. "I don't like that they can't interview these people. What the hell is this husband's story? He left with the dog! No calls between them all day, now he runs out and hires a criminal attorney. Sounds a little suspicious to me." He lifted his eyebrows as he spoke.

Mike was sitting at the table; he looked up at Bob. "If you have nothing to hide, you come forward," he stated flatly. Mike was visibly exhausted.

"It's just crazy. I don't understand that all these people can just refuse to speak to the police; this is a homicide investigation." Joe was agitated but trying not to get Mike upset.

Bob, Joe, and Jeanne were all in a difficult position. The tragedy had left Mike and his sisters totally devastated; unfortunately, it had also left them feeling totally vulnerable. The media was coming at them in droves and the story of the accident, now classified a homicide, was taking some very strange twists. It was hard for them to even imagine that anyone would be trying to cover up how this tragedy had occurred; they were too immersed in sorrow to believe it was possible. Bob was good at explaining things in a way that they could absorb slowly, presenting different options, no matter how unrealistic. Joe and Jeanne went with pure logic. They didn't waste time trying to explain away the obvious; the puzzle piece fits or it doesn't, they reasoned—turning it around and upside down still won't make it fit.

Jeanne and Marge came out. Roseann followed with the coffee.

"Apparently, you can just refuse to speak to the police," Jeanne said. She had been disappointed with the meeting with the DA. She believed Daniel Schuler had known that his wife was drinking when he had left the campground on the morning of the accident, and nothing at the meeting with the DA had convinced her otherwise.

"Well so far, nothing makes sense," Marge added. Marge was calm, quiet, and nonjudgmental. She and her husband had been a good match. Joe was all Bronx—streetwise, no-nonsense, and protective, yet in spite of his body builder's appearance, he was a real softie. Their kids were a combination of both: two boys looked like Marge, two looked like Joe, and their daughter was a combination of both. They were all good kids, polite and respectful.

"I had expected more information, and I definitely did not expect to hear that they were having trouble questioning the other families," Roseann said. "I understand that everyone is in shock, but that should make them want more answers. But I thought the investigators seemed anxious to get some answers, "she added.

"Yes, I believe the assistant district attorney used the word 'liars.' That's not a very good sign," Jeanne said.

"Knowing that they have already hired attorneys is putting a new twist on this. Why would they feel the need to do that?" Joe asked.

"I have a feeling that there is a lot more to this story, and I felt like the police investigators also have that feeling. A lot of lives have been lost here," Bob said.

"Yes, I thought it was very strange that Jackie asked for a divorce the next morning. Most couples end up split after losing a child because it becomes a constant reminder, but this sounds as if she is blaming her husband, and you have to wonder why."

"Yeah, maybe something with those cell phone calls he took," Joe said. "Maybe she does know he talked to Diane."

"The focus of the investigation is on the two men. Diane Schuler is already dead," Bob said.

"I hope Jackie Hance can survive this. I think I would just have a total breakdown," Marge said, sounding sincere.

"I agree. I can't even look at the pictures of her girls; it is devastating," Jeanne said.

"And it was her sister-in-law that caused this," Bob said.

"Eventually, she will be the one that comes forward and clears up the mystery here. No way is she burying her children without getting the truth," Jeanne said.

"Maybe she already knows," Joe said.

"Then she will be talking to the investigators," Jeanne said.

"Don't be so sure," Bob answered.

The conversations continued with an occasional comment from the grandsons and even some laughter. As hard as they tried to stray however, the conversation always came back to the Tragedy on the Taconic. It was consuming all of their lives.

****

On August 5th Investigator James Boyle was contacted by attorney Dominick Barbara who stated that he represents Daniel Schuler and that the following day he will be holding a press conference at 1 pm at his office in Garden City. Barbara told Boyle that he was invited to attend the conference and that Daniel Schuler would speak to Boyle afterwards. Barbara added that Daniel Schuler will answer any questions that Boyle may have. Boyle told Barbara that he will attend the conference and that he would very much like to speak with Daniel Schuler.

Also on this day, the day after the police had told the DA and the victims' families that the Hances were not talking, the Hance family released a statement that they were "shocked and saddened, we would never knowingly allow our daughters to travel with someone who might jeopardize their safety. This raises more questions than it provides answers."

13

Schuler Press Conference

August 6, 2009

The Bastardis' expected things to start to calm down the day after their meeting with the DA. They had all been through a lot in the past ten days. They continued to gather at Grandpa's house just because they always had and it wasn't something they were ready to give up. There was a comfort in everyone being there together.

The newspaper headlines were mild today: "Husband will seek to exhume body." That was news they liked. Diane Schuler's husband had been denying that she drank or smoked pot. He was not cooperating with the police and had already hired an attorney—not just any attorney but the transplant attorney, Dominic Barbara. Barbara was famous for a divorce case in which the husband, who had donated a kidney to his wife, was seeking millions of dollars in compensation for the kidney. For Daniel Schuler, Barbara had already arranged for a press conference scheduled for later that day.

The Bastardi family sat in the living room to view the press conference. Daniel Schuler walked out stone-faced. He looked very angry—not sad, but definitely angry. His hand was interlocked with the hand of his brother's wife (Jay Schuler), and the babysitter followed close behind. Dominic Barbara started by telling the group gathered before him that although he did not see any real benefit in it, his client, Daniel Schuler, wanted to talk about his wife and some of the events leading up to the tragedy on July 26.

Following the introductions, the ever-changing story started. First, the audience heard that the everyday mom had coffee before she left the campsite, that the Schulers had no marital problems, that Diane was not an alcoholic and rarely even drank (but just happened to have a bottle of Absolut vodka and some marijuana with her that day). Barbara sarcastically said that nine witnesses had seen her that morning, not drunk, with no alcohol or pot breath.

Then Barbara gave everyone a look at his medical expertise. He announced that Diane Schuler had numerous medical problems, which disregarded the fact that Daniel Schuler, Warren Hance, and Jay Schuler had initially told police during the interview at Westchester County Medical Center that Diane had no medical problems and was in excellent health. Barbara claimed that Diane Schuler had had an abscessed tooth for about two months. An abscessed tooth on the left side of her mouth, Barbara said, pointing to the left side of his mouth and asked Daniel Schuler for confirmation. Daniel acknowledged yes, the left side. Diane also had diabetes, and a lump on her leg that moved, Barbara continued. None of this had shown up on the autopsy report, and all of it was news to the medical examiner. (Most of what Barbara said in this press conference was actually news to the medical profession.) The Schuler family had not decided whether there would be another autopsy, Barbara claimed.

Now it was time for the reporters to ask questions. Barbara announced that he would not allow any questions about marijuana use "*at all*," because Daniel Schuler worked as a public safety officer under the Nassau County Police. He stated that marijuana use was not even a crime but a public health violation. This ignored the facts that, depending on the quantity someone possesses, it can be a felony and that smoking pot in front of children is still, at the least, endangering the welfare of a child—not to forget that driving while impaired is a crime.

The first reporter asked Daniel Schuler, "*Why* did you go up in separate cars?" Daniel responded that he had gone up a day earlier to open up the camper and "get a little fishing in."

The next reporter asked Daniel, "How do you explain her behavior that morning?"

Daniel shrugged and answered, "As normal. She was fine, had a cup of coffee in the morning, packed the cars up like we always do, and headed out, just like every other weekend."

Barbara quickly interrupted to add, "I might tell you that my investigators have already interviewed people at the campsite. No one saw her that morning with alcohol, drunk, acting strange, no pot breath..."

Barbara's private detective Thomas Ruskin, leaned forward and whispered to Barbara, then Ruskin leaned in to the microphone, saying, "It was the opposite."

Barbara nodded and continued with a pathetic look of excitement. "The opposite: happy, talking to people, gave a kiss good-bye to the owner of the camp, and that person smelled her breath. There was definitely no alcohol when she left that campground."

At that, Bobby looked at Mike and Joe and said, "I don't like the way this is starting." Joe nodded. Mike didn't move; he just sat there, tense.

Jeanne looked over at Bobby, shaking her head, and said, "That Barbara hops around like a little animated figure."

The reporters started to step up the questions, with the next reporter asking Daniel Schuler, "The police found a bottle of vodka in the van. Can you explain the bottle of vodka?"

With a dumb look, Daniel simply responded, "Don't know."

The next question was also asked of Daniel: "Are you saying that a medical condition caused her to drink?"

Of course, Dominic Barbara jumped in to answer. "Well, we don't know. Did she have a stroke and then have alcohol? If you believe the circumstances the way they are now described, you have to believe that a woman with five children in a car is smoking pot and drinking out of a bottle."

Joe looked at Bobby, asking, "Did I hear that right? What is he trying to say?" Bobby shrugged. Not only did the Bastardi family believe that, but the medical examiner had proved it; what the family couldn't believe was that Diane Schuler was defendable to anyone.

Barbara then rambled on about phone calls and a mystery witness. "She's on one side of the road, she goes over the divider, she goes back over, these are not the actions of a person that is just drunk. Something happened. He rambles some more.

"Yes, something happened; she smoked pot too," Mike's nephew Danny said. Mike's other nephews laughed.

"They sound like the actions of a drunk to me," nephew Mikey said.

Another reporter started to ask questions pertaining to the cell phone calls that were reported. "Do you know the conversation Emma had on cell?"

At this, Daniel Schuler's sister-in-law Jay, interrupted and ran through a few conversations that she claimed the nine-year-old victim Emma had with her father Warren Hance, on Diane Schuler's cell phone two hours prior to the accident. Jay stated, "She said everything was fine, that they had a great time." She was cut short by Barbara interrupting.

Thomas Ruskin stepped up to the microphone again. "What I think is important here is that our investigation shows inconsistencies in the reporting of this incident. We now know that there were four calls, know where calls went. We're following up on trying to determine what was said, was she at all confused..."

Because cell phone calls are not recorded and there were *no voice mails,* they were never going to be able to verify who was actually on Diane's cell phone or what was said in any of the calls.

For someone whom Barbara claimed wanted to speak about his wife, Daniel Schuler was letting everyone else answer for him. For nearly any question that was asked, someone other than Daniel jumped in to answer. The reporters who asked the tougher questions, Barbara just ignored.

One reporter asked Daniel how he would like his wife to be remembered, and Daniel answered, "She was a perfect wife, outstanding mother; reliable, trustworthy. I would marry her again tomorrow."

This was followed by a reporter asking Daniel, "What did you think when you received the toxicology report?" At this, everyone jumped in to help Daniel answer.

Jay Schuler shook her head and said, "Not true."

Daniel started to say it was not true, but Barbara interrupted to say, "I have not given him the report yet." Of course by now, the newspapers had already released the information contained in the report.

Moving quickly off the real topic, Barbara suggested that the reporters ask questions about Daniel's wife, his nieces, and his son and daughter.

At this suggestion, Jay Schuler came back to take the stage, to tell the wonderful things about Diane, to say that the toxicology report was not true and there had to be another explanation. "No way would she jeopardize children."

It seemed to Mike's family as if "jeopardize" was a gross understatement.

After what seemed like an eternity, the press conference was wrapping up. The Bastardis had learned that medical forensics was no match for the Schulers, their attorney, or their private investigator. Daniel Schuler ended the conference by pointing and announcing in an accusatory voice, "Listen to this: my heart is clear, she didn't drink, she's not an alcoholic; did you get that? I go to bed every night knowing my heart is clear."

When the press conference ended, the Bastardis were all stunned. This was bizarre.

Bobby stood up and faced the rest of the family. "What the hell was that?" He was angry. "We already know she was drunk *that* day."

Joe was shaking his head. "Unbelievable! Un-freakin'-believable."

Jeanne had been watching Mike during the news conference. He had been very quiet and focused on the TV. She had seen him rubbing his hands together, a sign that he was nervous. She asked, "Mike, you okay?"

Mike stood up. He was shaking his head, and he spoke slowly. "Are they kidding me? I *absolutely* can't believe what I just heard. Did anybody tell them that seven innocent people are already dead? That she was driving, the autopsy and toxicology reports are complete."

"I can't believe what I just saw." Marge was upset, and she looked like she was going to burst out crying. "Had coffee, kissed good-bye, then why didn't she call him when she felt sick?"

Roseann was furious. "What kind of people are they? I can't even make any sense out of this." Her voice was shaking. "Did I just hear them say she wasn't drunk, it's a mistake?" Her voice was getting higher.

Everyone walked out to the patio to smoke, even those who didn't smoke. The older kids were there too. The boys were furious; there was a lot of talking going on between them, and it sounded pretty ugly. What an incredible insult to those who had lost their grandfather and uncle at the same time because of a drunk and high driver.

"I was expecting them to come out and say they were just as shocked as we were and offer some apology or something." Mike was upset. "Not a word makes any sense."

"Jeanne, why are you so quiet?" Marge asked.

"I'm trying to process this. That was too bizarre. Look at who was there: a sister-in-law, no brother, a babysitter—where did she come from and why? A controversial defense lawyer, his private investigator—what is he investigating? Apparently, they are focused on relieving Daniel Schuler of any responsibility, and if that's the best defense they have, it's obvious to me he is guilty of something."

"That's called setting up your defense," Bob stated. "Why does he have a lawyer already? He must think he needs one."

"How do you go on TV and refuse questions about the pot, say you know nothing about the vodka, everything was fine, and there has to be a mistake?" Marge asked. "I can't believe this!"

"Okay, let's go over this," Roseann said, looking at Jeanne. "They said she didn't drink, it's a mistake."

"Yes, even though they found a bottle of vodka in her car and an extra six grams of vodka in her stomach, "Jeanne said.

"Let's not forget the 0.19% alcohol blood level," Joe added.

"She would never jeopardize the children's safety?" Roseann asked.

"Yes, even though her daughter and three nieces have been killed," Jeanne answered.

"She had a stroke lasting four hours, drove around. Somehow the medical examiner found no illness but he found alcohol and marijuana in her system, body fluids, and stomach?" Roseann continued.

"Yes and there is no explanation for how she obtained alcohol or pot while having this stroke and all," Jeanne said, "and they are not answering questions about that."

"Or maybe a toothache caused this," Joe said.

"And Daniel is not cooperating with the police because he is grieving and busy at the hospital, even though he took time off for a press conference," Roseann said.

"Is it me, or did Schuler seem angry, like he was blaming everyone at the press conference?" Marge asked.

"No, it's not you," Bob said. "Guilt works that way. I imagine the state police and the medical examiner's office are wondering what that was all about too."

Mike had stayed quiet. Everything had hit him as a direct personal insult. He stood there looking at the rest of his family, his hands in his pockets. "Perfect, outstanding?" he asked. "He's describing my father, not the drunk that killed him." He walked away.

It was clear to the family that the press conference had focused on showing that Daniel Schuler had had no idea his wife drank or smoked pot and no idea where she would get vodka, and that he had not believed his wife was drunk; thus relieving him of any responsibility for leaving her at the campsite with the children.

****

Investigator Boyle and Investigator Shannon Morrison arrived at Garden City and watched the press conference. After the conference Investigator Boyle introduced himself to Dominick Barbara. Barbara said that he and Daniel would talk to them soon and had Boyle and Morrison sit in a waiting room for about twenty minutes. Barbara then entered the room and informed them that Daniel had to leave, and no interview would take place today.

Investigators Boyle and Morrison then met with Warren Hance and his attorney Doug Hayden at Hayden's office in Uniondale, NY. Boyle interviewed Warren Hance in reference to the phone calls made to him on July 26th from Diane Schuler. Hance stated that at approximately 9am he received a call from his daughter Emma who said they would be home by 1pm and that everyone had a great time. Hance stated that he received a second call at his office at about 11:30am. During this call Diane Schuler said that they would be home closer to 1:30pm. Diane sounded fine at the time. At approximately 1pm Diane called Warren's home phone and spoke to Jackie Hance. Jackie Hance reported to Warren that Diane sounded "out of it" and that she heard kids crying in the background. Warren then called Diane who sounded incoherent. He asked Diane to put Emma on the phone, when Emma got on the phone she sounded upset and stated that she saw signs for Sleepy Hollow and Tarrytown. Warren then spoke to Diane and told her to pull over and he will come and get her. (A different account from his first interview)

14

Conflicting Stories

August 6, 2009

The press conference was not the only surprise on this day. The *New York Post* ran this headline on the cover: "Taconic Tragedy ON THE ROCKS Killer Mom's boozy rants on marriage." The article stated

> The Long Island mother who drove bombed out of her mind with a minivan full of kids routinely bellied up at the bar and griped about her failing marriage and stressful job, a drinking buddy told the post. "She recently seemed under pressure like work and family was getting to her," said the pal. "Her marriage seemed a bit rocky and, and I think she felt trapped by it. For the last couple of months she didn't appear to be a happy woman. I wouldn't say she was an alcoholic, but she liked her drinks. She liked her vodka."
>
> Diane Schuler crashed four hours after leaving an upstate camp ground in Sullivan County NY.
>
> A caller to WABC/Channel 7 said the campground at Hunters Lake—where Schuler and her family regularly

> stayed—is a known boozing area, where wild parties are the norm.

Ann Scott, the owner of the campground told a different story. Another article, was released on August 6 stating

> "The rules around here are strict. Campers who drink outside their campsites are to be evicted. The guide rule is if you abuse it you lose it and you're out of here," Scott said. "I don't ever remember seeing her with a drink. I don't ever remember smelling alcohol on her."
>
> Maybe not, but Eyewitness News heard from a viewer who spent the last ten years as a seasonal camper at Hunter Lake. He claims he noticed a lot of drinking at least in years past. "It was not for me that's for sure. How people could do that pretty much every weekend still amazes me." (RV Business)

****

The original statement Daniel Schuler gave to police on July 31 stated that he and his wife had drunk on Friday night at the campsite and that his wife smoked marijuana once in a while. His sister-in-law Jay Schuler had confirmed in her statement to police that Diane Schuler smoked pot regularly.

The district attorney in Sullivan County can elect to have a grand jury if there is reason to believe that Daniel Schuler knew that his wife was drinking but left her there with the children on July 26. It was therefore possible that Ann Scott was not truthful, to relieve herself of any culpability or bad publicity.

15
Talk Shows and News Shows

August 7, 2009

The Taconic Tragedy continued to make headlines in several newspapers. Daniel Schuler's flat-out denial of his wife's drinking and pot smoking and his rejection of the toxicology report at the press conference were shocking. According to the *New York Post:*

> Schuler's lawyer Dominic Barbara had several bizarre explanations for the horrific crash. They included a possible stroke, a prior case of gestational diabetes, a two month old abscessed tooth, and a lump on her leg that was moving. Dominic Barbara backed off reports that Schuler would have his wife's body exhumed. Meanwhile Schuler yesterday refused to meet with state police investigators for a scheduled interview about the case.
>
> The toxicology report found that Diane Schuler had a blood alcohol level of .19, six grams (the equivalent of ten shots) of unabsorbed alcohol in her stomach, 113 n/ml of THC (active component in marijuana) in her blood, to all of which Daniel Schuler said "not true". Authorities found a

> 1.75 liter bottle of Absolut Vodka in the van she had been driving. An autopsy found that Diane Schuler had NOT suffered a stroke, heart attack, or aneurysm and was NOT suffering from diabetes and the Westchester County medical examiner's office stood by its findings yesterday.

For the next several weeks, the Taconic Tragedy was on almost every news, morning, and talk show. Panels of experts weighed in. The public was fascinated with the story. It was inconceivable to viewers that a mother could have caused this much death and disaster. What was even more fascinating, however, was that her family defended her actions and tried to blame a variety of nonexistent medical conditions for her behavior.

The photographs of the accident were hard to look at; scattered on the ground in them, the array of small white sheets told a horrific story. The families not cooperating with the police told another.

Various medical experts, doctors, psychologists and others weighed in on a variety of talk shows, news channels, and phone calls. Some spoke on closest drinkers. CNN news had a clinical psychologist on one such show. "There is no way that he didn't know his wife had a problem. You cannot live with someone who can hide that level of drinking and marijuana use effectively," the expert said. Having spent two days in a one room camper, the Bastardi family ruled out the possibility that Daniel Schuler didn't know. It was not denial; it was a guilty defense.

The autopsy had found that Schuler's liver appeared healthy, of a normal consistency, and with no unusual fat deposits or scarring. "It doesn't mean you can rule out alcoholism," said Dr. Mary Case, chief medical examiner of St Louis County, Missouri. "Alcoholism is often not detectable in relatively young, well-nourished adults." Diane Schuler was 5'2" and 204 pounds.

The office of the Westchester County medical examiner stated that the marijuana, with that high reading would have grossly intensified the effects of the alcohol.

Legal experts also weighed in on the tragedy. Jeanine Pirro, who had formerly served as the Westchester County District Attorney for twelve years, weighed in on the Taconic Tragedy for various news shows.

When interviewed by Fox News, Judge Pirro was clear to put the blame on Diane Schuler, who, she said, "clearly has a drinking problem." Pirro had no pity for Diane Schuler, her husband, or her brother. Diane's husband, Pirro said, "left from the same location, in a separate car with the dog, which makes us wonder what happened that day." Pirro's main focus was on Daniel Schuler, who, she said, "did not have the intelligence to stop her before she intentionally got in that minivan intoxicated, and her brother, who, after talking to her on a cell phone, only told the police she was having trouble with her vision. Instead of saying, 'My sister is disoriented,' he should have said, 'She is drunk and high!' There are a lot of questions to be answered, and we all wonder and hope this will come to light and give all of the victims' families' closure."

Jeanine Pirro's advice: "Throw everybody in the grand jury under penalty of perjury."

Mike watched every show that he could. He spent countless hours on the internet, reading interviews, following the story, and talking to lawyers and investigators. He was trying hard to make sense out of the senseless, to get answers that weren't coming, to try to find some peace that he would not find.

16
The Anbesol Theory

August 13, 2009

A new day, a new excuse. Anbesol caused the wrong-way driver DWI crash that killed eight people...according to the newest absurd explanation presented by attorney Dominic Barbara on August 13th.The Anbesol theory said that Diane Schuler's blood alcohol content was so high because she used Anbesol for her toothache.

The spokesperson for Wyeth, the manufacturer of Anbesol, immediately set the record straight, as did various medical experts. Anbesol has small amounts of benzyl alcohol, which dissolves immediately after application. Dr. Michael Baden, New York City's former chief medical examiner, stated, "There is a tiny bit of alcohol in Anbesol, but it is a different type than you would find in Vodka or hard liquor; that's ethyl alcohol."

Mike and Jeanne were on their way to Yonkers to meet his family for lunch at Grandpa's house when they heard the news flash about the Anbesol theory. Jeanne just shook her head. "I can't believe what I am hearing. Is there no limit to this lunatic? He can just come out with all this crap on the news?"

"There are rules of ethics for lawyers. I don't know how he gets away with it," Mike answered, his face showing his agitation. Mike pulled the car into the cul-de-sac and, looking at the other cars, said, "I guess they are all here already." Jeanne nodded, and they went up the steps and into the house. They were greeted by Roseann, who asked if they wanted coffee.

Jeanne nodded and said, "Yes, unless you have any Anbesol."

There was some laughing, and Bobby stood up to greet Mike. "So, I guess you've heard the new theory?" he asked.

Mike nodded and said, "And I am starting to take this real personal."

"It's in the newspaper," Bob said, pointing to the neatly stacked pile of papers on the table. Mike picked up the pile, and the two men went out to the patio to join the others already outside.

"Do you believe this?" Marge asked, looking at Jeanne.

"I cannot make sense out of anything," Jeanne answered. "As if the toxicology report wasn't bad enough, now the Schuler family wants to explain it away."

"I am starting to think that they have a lot to hide," Roseann said. "Why else would they be saying these ridiculous things and making excuses for her? She just killed four of their children."

"We saw Jeanine Pirro on the news. She was very clear in saying that there should be a grand jury," Jeanne said.

"Well, that's good. Then maybe the DA will do that," Marge said.

The women went out to join the others gathered on the patio.

Roseann sat at the table and addressed the group. "We were talking about meeting with the Hances,"she said.

Jeanne turned around. "Who's we? And meet for what?" she asked.

"All of us, or whoever wants to do that," Roseann answered.

"I heard there was something in the newspaper about that, but I thought it was a wild story," Jeanne said, glancing at Mike. "What is it you want to meet about?"

"We all lost so much; they lost their three children—just for comfort, grieving," Roseann said, adding, "I understand that they stopped speaking to Daniel Schuler after his press conference."

"How could they ever speak to him again?" Marge commented.

"We have no idea what really went on that day, and both men have hired attorneys. I am not interested in meeting," Jeanne stated. "I am still expecting Jackie Hance to talk to the investigators. I can't believe she would put up with what Daniel Schuler is doing and just let it go. It is the woman that killed her daughters that he is talking about," Jeanne added.

"Imagine how she must feel to hear these stories," Marge said.

"No, I actually can't," Roseann said.

"Listen to this," Bob said, looking at the *New York Post.* "Warren Hance was enraged that Daniel Schuler concocted a bizarre medical excuse to explain his wife's condition and denied her drinking problem. The Hance family attorney James McCrorie did not deny that his clients will no longer associate with the Schulers. That was supposed to be confidential, he said."

"Well that puts another twist," Bob said.

"It certainly does, coming from the man that keeps insisting that he thought his sister *was* having a medical emergency, that lied to the police and continues to do so," Jeanne said.

"The pot calling the kettle black," Marge said.

"Well, like I said, a meeting would be premature," Jeanne said.

The conversation changed as the grandchildren started arriving for lunch.

17

Dining Out

August 2009

It was mid-August, a clear and warm Saturday night, with no humidity. Mike and Jeanne were meeting Irving Anolik and his wife, Evelyn for dinner in Rockland. The Anoliks frequented certain restaurants in which they had a special table reserved and in some, their own wait staff. This was the first time Mike had gone out since the accident and Jeanne was grateful that Irving had invited them. She knew Mike wouldn't have gone out otherwise; he was having a really hard time since the accident.

Tonight was to be Italian food. Mike and Jeanne arrived at the restaurant right on time and were escorted to the Anoliks' table, where the other couple was already seated. Jeanne noticed a few people looking at their table and whispering. The accident had been all over the news and so had pictures of Irving and Mike. Mike either didn't notice or didn't care; in either case, Jeanne was relieved. She doubted Mike would be rattled with Irving there anyway.

The food was delicious. It brought back memories of the homemade pasta Mike's mother used to make. There was nothing quite as good as his mom's pasta but the food here was a close second.

Irving and Mike briefly discussed business and Irving told Mike that, once again, they would all be meeting with the district attorney. He brought Mike up to date and discussed some options that they might have for learning more about the events of July 26 and for pursuing legal action. A civil suit would allow them the ability to subpoena any person who had been involved with the accident in some way but who was not cooperating with the police. Irving absolutely saw the need for a grand jury; with neither the Schuler nor Hance family completely cooperating with police investigators there was reason for suspicion. Irving explained to Mike the circumstances that could make involved persons also culpable: Anyone who had been aware of Diane Schuler's drinking that day or who had supplied the alcohol or marijuana could face criminal charges and possibly be charged as an accomplice.

Finally, the conversation went on to more pleasant topics. Irving, a graduate of Harvard, had had an illustrious career as an attorney and always had interesting stories to tell. His wife was highly intelligent and equally as interesting and together they could also be quite comical. They were very family oriented people, and Evelyn brought Jeanne up to date on her and Irving's family. The Bastardis had been guests at both of their granddaughters' weddings, and now there was a grandchild. In turn, Jeanne brought the Anoliks up to date on her own family.

The time flew by, and the couples had been at the restaurant for several hours before they realized. Jeanne was relieved to see how relaxed Mike was. Irving was a good friend and had been shielding Mike from the media. He had been tireless in answering all the reporters and television appearances.

Jeanne did not want the night to end. It was such a relief to feel good again, if only for the night. It was late and time to leave, however. Irving and Evelyn said the couples would get together again soon. They were true to their word.

18
Bad Days

August 15, 2009

It seemed like the family took turns having bad days. Today was obviously Jeanne's. There was the usual flow of people in Grandpa's house, a mix of friends and relatives. The women were gathered around the kitchen table when Jeanne and Mike arrived. As they walked in, Roseann announced that Brian Schuler had been released from the hospital. Mike stopped, standing with his hands in his pockets; he waited for Roseann to continue. "He is being moved to a rehabilitation center," she said. Mike nodded his acknowledgment and walked toward the patio.

"That's the news," Jeanne replied as she kept walking.

Roseann looked shocked. "He's just a little boy; it's not his fault," she snapped.

"Is there coffee?" Jeanne asked, looking at the pot on the counter and ignoring the remark.

Joey's wife, Christina, was already pouring her a cup and handed it to her with a smile and that little laugh she had. Jeanne took the cup, thanked Christina, and walked out to the patio, the others following her. Jeanne adored Christina. She was the kind of girl any mom would handpick to marry her son. Jeanne was glad her nephew had married Christina.

Jeanne joined the group that was already sitting on the patio. Grabbing a pastry, she greeted the others. Like her brothers-in-law, Jeanne was exhausted and stressed. They were watching their spouses and children suffer the unthinkable. Trying to get their family through something like this meant trying to put their own grief on hold. Mike was waking up screaming in his sleep, their daughter was crying in her sleep and having nightmares, and their son was barely sleeping at all. Last night had been one of those nights when Ike had barely slept.

"I guess you heard about the little boy?" Bob said, laughing.

"Yes. So are the police going to question him now? Oh no, don't tell me, the lawyer says he's too traumatized?" Jeanne asked.

"Well, he has been through a trauma," Roseann answered.

"Yes, he has," Jeanne said as she turned around to answer. "And nothing is *ever* going to change that. I think the detectives are smart enough and experienced enough to handle that. They deal with trauma every day. He is also the only living witness to that entire weekend."

"No, I think you can count out questioning the boy. They can't even question the father," Bob answered with a laugh.

"Of course, because a five-year-old can say, 'Mommy and Daddy had a fight,'" Bobby Jr. added.

"Or 'Mommy's smoke smells funny,'" Richie N. said, laughing.

Jeanne softened. "Of course I'm happy for the poor little boy. It's a miracle anyone survived. We can all thank god for that, not his parents." She paused. "I *do* resent that Daniel Schuler is getting back the only survivor. He doesn't deserve any more than the dog he left with. I hope child protective services take that child and place him with a relative. Then he'll at least have a chance. I will *never* believe that he drove away not knowing that anything was wrong. To me, he is as guilty as her, and that doesn't make him a very good father. Do you really think that child has a chance with him as his father?"

"No, Aunt Jeanne, genetically speaking, his chances of abusing drugs and alcohol are pretty high," her nephew Richie G. said. The boys were joking.

"Wait 'til he can use the internet and see the story himself!"Mikey said.

"I agree with Jeanne," Joe said, looking at Bob. "She was probably drunk and high all weekend. Maybe she was still drunk from the night before. Those were some high readings, and some still in her stomach," he added.

"There is a lot of speculation and a lot of talk. One thing I keep hearing is that Diane found out that her husband was having an affair and they were fighting," Bob answered.

Joe was sitting across from Mike. "Yeah, I heard he was banging a sister-in-law or babysitter, banging somebody; did you hear that?" Joe asked as he twirled a cigar in his fingers. "Heard it wasn't the first time, either. Some called it common knowledge, said the police know too," he added.

Bob laughed. "Well, I guess that could put you over the edge." Bob always tried to deliver the news calmly and when possible, with a little humor. He knew a lot of people and always seemed to come up with some new information.

"That's one explanation: the husband wanted out so bad, he just drove away and never looked back," Jeanne added.

Joe and Jeanne thought a lot alike. Things were black and white, and they didn't want it sugarcoated. They did not have the capacity to deny logic and reason, or the patience to try.

"Maybe that's why there weren't any cell calls between Diane and her husband, even when she was so late getting home" Marge added.

"He changed his story about going up to the campground on Thursday when the troopers got the E-Z Pass records and discovered he went up on Friday, so where do you think he was on Thursday and why would he tell the police that?" Bob added.

"Oh yeah, that fishing-trip story." Joe smiled. "Yeah, Schuler told the police he went up there on Thursday, a day earlier, to fish. He hired a lawyer, and all of a sudden, he says he went up on Friday and no one has asked him why he was lying about going up early."

"Yes, that was his answer to why they had separate cars on their family weekend, and when the E-Z Pass record was pulled, he just changed his story," Bob said.

"He said that he went up on Thursday at his press conference too," Roseann added.

"Well, with his wife dead, who can really say if it was Thursday or Friday? Maybe his wife figured out he was missing on Thursday. That could have started off their weekend and might get her drinking. For that matter, how many people do you really think believe that was the first day that woman drank or smoked pot? Maybe he's a drunk, who knows? They go upstate to camp and do what?" Joe was shaking his head.

"But, that's all it is right now, talk," Bob said. "The detectives aren't stupid. Even if they think or *know* that the Schulers' are all liars, it doesn't mean that they can prove it. Why do you think he found that lawyer? Look at his past clients."

"If Ruskin was really there to investigate, he should be exhuming the body and doing lab tests. Finding a few people who say nice things about her isn't going to clear shit up," Joe added.

"He's not investigating jack! Maybe it's as simple as it appears: Daniel Schuler just wanted out." Jeanne looked at Bob and Joe. "You don't really believe all those cheating and divorce stories are all lies, do you? We've heard that too many times, from too many people, and he lost all creditability when he hired Dominic Barbara. Innocent, grieving husbands cooperate. Guilty people hire lawyers and hide. He got the lawyer for *himself*," Jeanne said.

"That's why there should be a grand jury," Mike added, walking to the table. "Too many questions and not enough answers. They ran out and hired lawyers the day after the toxicology report came in. What does that tell you?" Mike spoke quietly. "The detectives said none of them were really answering questions. Why would you act like that if you had nothing to hide?"

He wasn't really asking a question.

19
Bad Nights

Mid-August 2009

It was one of those stifling hot nights that had followed a relatively quiet day. Mike and Jeanne had been at home and were grateful that they had not been hit with any new news flashes. As evening approached, they ate dinner out on the patio. Then they watched some television and went up to bed. Jeanne stayed up to read, and it seemed as though she had just fallen asleep when she heard Mike screaming, "No, no!" She jumped up and turned on the light. Mike sat up, looking startled. His head was soaking wet. He covered his face with both hands and Jeanne realized he was shaking all over. As she spoke to him, his eyes filled with tears.

"I still can't believe this. How could someone have done this to my family? And of all the cars on the road, how could it have been theirs?"

They went downstairs and sat at the table and Mike started to calm down. This was not the first night that Mike had been jolted from what appeared to be a sound sleep. Jeanne suspected it was also far from the last. It seemed as though Mike slept only from sheer exhaustion and that on any other night, sleep was only temporary for him. He often awoke in this panicked state, reliving a dream or nightmare that had jarred his sleep. When Mike had a peaceful night, it was their son who came in crying from some nightmare.

Mike stared straight ahead. "This whole story does not make any sense to me. Witnesses saw Diane Schuler vomiting and driving like a lunatic as early as 11:30. There were four cell phone calls after that, and I'm being told that not one person she talked to could tell she was drunk. I don't believe it. Aside from all the lies, she had the vodka and pot with her. That's a coincidence?" Jeanne just nodded. "The police, the district attorney's office, they all said the Schuler's and Hances were liars, that they were not cooperating, they ran out to get lawyers. It's not as easy for me to give up as it is for the police. I want to know every lie and who is saying them. I want to know what really happened that day. I want to see everyone's phone bill who talked to her that day, and I want all Diane's credit card records. I want to know if there were calls going on between the family members. I want to know if that woman could have been stopped *before* she killed my family and all those children." Mike paused. "Maybe I should get my own investigators," he said, looking at Jeanne. Jeanne nodded again.

Jeanne often wondered if life would ever be good again. Was it even possible to recover from such a shock and put the pieces together again? Sometimes, it just didn't seem possible. She knew it would never happen with the constant news reports. This was a long road ahead of them, she thought.

20
Second Meeting with the DA

August 18, 2009

The Bastardi family had been called for another meeting at the district attorney's office. They had hoped they would be getting new information or a grand jury. This time, they had a lot of questions. They all arrived separately with high hopes of getting some good news.

At the meeting, they were informed that the investigators had *not* gotten the information they had wanted. The family had not been forthcoming, and the police did not have adequate access to Daniel Schuler. Jackie Hance had never been interviewed. The McDonalds' video had not shown that Diane Schuler was clearly drunk. The Schulers' camper had not been searched at the campground. No guest list from the camp had been obtained. The attendants at Sunoco had refused to speak to the police. They had no answers about the marijuana or even the vodka, such as where they had come from or why Daniel Schuler kept changing the story about them.

Jackie Hance was just not ever going to talk to the police or give a statement. We had hoped that at some point she would be the one to shed some light on the case. After all, most people were still stunned that a mother could load her van with kids and cause the worst accident in 75 years in Westchester County, and Jackie Hance *had lost her* children. We had expected that Jackie would be seeking justice with a vengeance. All the family knew was that according to news reports, the Hance and Schuler families had stopped talking after the toxicology report had been released.

"Did you interview Jackie Hance yet?" Roseann asked.

"No, we can't. We're told she can't talk about it. There could be a suicide concern," one state trooper said.

"You told us that the last time we were here," Jeanne said.

The other state trooper stared at her.

Jeanne stared back, unmoved. "She must want to know what happened by now. It's been all over the news that her husband Warren, had cell phone calls and that he repeatedly insisted Diane was sick, and now Jackie must know Diane was drunk and high. I don't understand why she is not asking to speak to the investigators."Jeanne understood how the Hances would be suffering, but she was afraid that their refusal to talk might allow Daniel Schuler to get away with a serious crime. Four children and three men were dead, and because those three men had died, *someone else on that highway was alive*. It could have been another family traveling with their children who had been hit and killed. Someone was inevitably going to die that day because of Diane Schuler. People had a right know if Diane could have been stopped and what really had happened during those four hours, and if Daniel Schuler had known she had been drinking.

"There's no way to say how a person will react in an emergency. It's not a crime, and Warren wasn't under oath when we questioned him," the trooper said. "The families have not been forthcoming."

"So there's no crime in lying to the police during a homicide investigation? Then we're back to why there should be a grand jury," Jeanne said. "There's no way to know how a person would react in an emergency that lasted four hours? We were told her brother knew she "wasn't feeling well" for two hours. He didn't know how to react for two hours? That's a long emergency."

The Bastardis were told that those were *moral issues* rather than *indictable offenses.*

"He lost his three children, and he has to live with that," someone added.

"Which is why I don't understand why he is not fully cooperating with you, or what exactly is he covering up?" Jeanne said. It was hard for her to see Mike so upset. He couldn't eat, sleep, or think about anything except the accident. He had expected answers, and he was entitled to them. He wanted to know if Diane Schuler could have been stopped. To the Bastardi family, the toxicology report was not disputable, and the medical emergency story therefore did nothing more than cover up the truth.

"So Warren Hance could be lying about all this, and Daniel Schuler isn't really being questioned, and he may have left her there with those children, knowing she was drinking and obviously smoking pot and you can't call for a grand jury?" Roseann asked, visibly upset. "What about witnesses from the campground? Like everyone that was ever there when they were. People have pictures, videos, or maybe speak to the police. There should be a complete guest list. There should be a grand jury to question these people."

"If new evidence comes up, that could change," the assistant DA said.

"It is not rational to believe that the Hances received that horrific news, were shocked to hear Diane Schuler would drink, and then just moved on. They won't cooperate with the investigation and they have *no questions for you*?" Jeanne asked, looking at the investigators. "He hired an attorney, took four cell phone calls that day, and that's it?" She was stunned.

No one answered.

"What about the pot? Daniel Schuler admitted his wife was a pot smoker. Her toxicology was extremely high; the drugs could have caused the crash. Daniel Schuler doesn't have to answer those questions either?" Roseann asked.

"His lawyer refuses to let him answer that," Investigator Boyle answered.

"Another reason for a grand jury," Jeanne said.

At this point, Irving and the other attorneys argued and discussed their views on a grand jury. The DA's office explained that at this time in a civil trial, the family had more options than the police did. Those involved could be called in for a deposition and be placed under oath. Records such as phone bills, cell phone records, credit cards, and the like could be subpoenaed.

The Bastardis kept hearing that the Hances would have to live with this the rest of their lives. Unfortunately, so would Mike's family. The Hances had lost all their children; the question that haunted the Bastardis was, *why?* Was it more important to protect Diane Schuler than to be honest with the police? Or who else were they protecting? If they kept quiet, Daniel Schuler might be getting away with a crime.

Mike and his family had left the first DA meeting with the investigation in full swing. They had been told that both Daniel Schuler and Warren Hance stood the possibility of being charged with crimes for their roles on the day of the accident. Keeping quiet and lying certainly had their advantages for the men, but the Bastardis were far from giving up on the possibility that Warren Hance would speak out and Daniel Schuler would face charges.

More questions and answers followed, then some talking and arguing between the attorneys. Mike and his sisters were drained and devastated. They had not had their questions answered. They were told again that they would get further with a civil suit than the police would get with their questions now that the Hance and Schuler families had hired attorneys.

This was not the way the family had expected that a homicide investigation would go.

The district attorney informed Mike's family that the only person who could be charged with a crime in this situation was Diane Schuler, and when she had died, the charges had died with her. Had she lived, she would have been charged for the seven deaths and the injury of her son.

The DA held a press conference to make the announcement.

To say the Bastardis' were shocked that the case was already being closed would be a gross understatement.

Mike felt terribly let down. He felt much gratitude toward the state police; he continued to believe that they were trying very hard to get to the bottom of this, that they wanted the truth as much as he did. He believed that the state police investigators were not ready to close the case, either. He was now relying on them to continue to investigate.

****

The New York State Police continued their investigation through November 2009.

21
People Magazine

August 24, 2009

Mike and his sisters were meeting at Grandpa's house in Yonkers for lunch. *People* magazine had come out with a story on the accident. Jeanne and Mike walked out to the patio. "How did you like the *People* magazine article?" Roseanne asked.

"It was okay," Mike answered. "It was really about Schuler."

"You, Jeanne?" Roseann asked.

"I really didn't like it. I can't take all this family-in-denial crap. I don't believe for one second that they're in denial; they just want to be relieved of responsibility. The reality is, she did it and she was drunk, and even if it's too horrific for them to be related to her, they can't change that," Jeanne said.

"I don't believe they're really in denial either," Marge said. "Her husband's probably just like her."

"No question about it, this is the way he gets away with any potential role in it. He didn't know anything, he didn't see anything. She's dead." Jeanne was disgusted.

"The one brother-in-law admits in the *People* article that they knew she smoked pot. The sister-in-law had already told that to the state police," Mike added.

"They're all a bunch of liars," Joe said, adding, "everybody that lies has a motive to lie, did you notice that? If Schuler played a role, he might not get his kid back, and like Irving said, he could face charges."

"Warren's another one; he had a few phone calls. He doesn't want anybody to think he could have done something to stop it and didn't, now that his kids are gone,"Jeanne said. "The way he hides from the investigators and ran out to get a lawyer, it just doesn't seem like he is so innocent or was so shocked by the toxicology report." she added.

"Yeah, she's right. Think about that," Joe said. "How many parents that lost their kids wouldn't be out looking for answers, wanting to know about the brother-in-law's role? He had every opportunity; that's why he won't even talk to the police."

"Well that's why nothing makes sense. None of them tell the same story twice, and it sounds ridiculous." Marge sounded really down.

"He may not have anticipated the outcome, but the results from his lapse in judgment affect more than just his family,"Jeanne added. "It's ludicrous that they don't have to answer questions for the police."

"I heard Warren Hances' lawyer called the state police saying Warren was upset that *People* magazine said his one daughter had been alive," Bob said.

"Well, he would have known that if they talked to the state police, everyone else knew. They went to see Jackie Hance and told whoever answered the door, some off-duty cop, that they didn't want to ask Jackie any questions, they just wanted to give her information, and the man at the door said, 'She doesn't want to see you,' and closed the door. Interesting they were surrounded in all these cops, isn't it?" Jeanne said.

"Yeah, for a couple of weeks, I heard, and the husband works under the police or something, like a security guard," Joe said.

"He works for the police and they didn't drug test him after this? After a homicide that killed seven people, committed by his drunken, druggie wife and knowing he was the last one with her?" Jeanne asked, looking disgusted.

"Say it isn't so, Bob," Joe said as he looked at Bob.

"Apparently it is so," Bob said.

"Well, the mother of the three girls must be totally destroyed, maybe suicidal," Marge said quietly.

"Which is exactly why I do not understand why she is refusing to speak to the investigators. No matter how hard it is, there's an overwhelming desire to hear what happened; you have a *need t*o know every detail, no matter how hard it is. You're telling me she didn't want to know who was with her children at that accident, or if they suffered? She just accepted that her sister-in-law was drunk for the first time and killed her children, and she had no questions for the police? Didn't you all want to know?" Jeanne asked.

"I did," Mike said, "every second, anything that they could tell me."

"Me, too," Marge agreed.

"Maybe Jackie Hance didn't even know about the cell phone calls," Roseann stated.

"Maybe not, who knows? Without a statement, we sure don't," Jeanne continued, "but if any of us were in Jackie Hance's position, do you believe that we would accept that story, that the rest of this family would just sit back and accept that story? She should be the one insisting on a grand jury! She has more reasons to want to know what really happened than anyone. I think when you get news like that and it was your sister-in-law, you would be demanding some answers from your husband and brother-in-law. I certainly would," Jeanne said with a shrug. "So why isn't she talking to the police? Asking them what *they* know? If she is not up to it, why isn't her family? Warren's family is obviously in no position; it was his sister."

"I totally agree with that," Joe said. "I would be knocking on Daniel's door."

Everyone nodded in agreement.

"Yeah, hold that thought, Joe," Jeanne answered. They all laughed.

"The news said child protective services are looking into Daniel Schuler," Bob stated.

"They definitely should be," Roseann said. "He admitted he knew his wife smoked pot to relieve the stress from the kids, and she was high that day with his kids in the car; why isn't that neglect? He now says he knew she traveled with the open bottle of vodka in the car, too. That should be enough for CPS; they're not limited to just that day."

"I hear Warren and Schuler haven't spoken since Schuler got that lawyer," Joe commented.

"Warren laid the groundwork by telling the police that Diane said she wasn't feeling well. Why didn't he just come forward? Say he panicked, say they had been through this before, say something! He kept adding to that not-feeling-well story—disoriented, vision problem…everything but drunk! I think they all have something on each other," Jeanne said.

"Let's hope we find out," Joe said. "You never know when someone might come forward."

Seeing that Marge was teary-eyed, Jeanne said, "In any event, Marge, if you take my kids out for any reason, I'm going to need a note from your dentist."

They laughed. The conversation changed.

22
Going Back to College

Late August 2009

Less than a month since the funerals, Mike and Jeanne had to drive their daughter back to college. It was going to be especially hard for Mike, but they had agreed that it would be better for their daughter to get back and get busy. Taija had been exceptionally quiet since the funerals. It wasn't necessarily a good thing, but that was her way. Jeanne knew her daughter was trying to block out the pain. Jeanne also knew that wouldn't work for very long but with Taija's friends and sorority sisters there with her, when the time came, Taija would have support. She had some good friends there.

They packed up two cars and headed off. The drive was better than usual, and it was always exciting to see the University Park campus. After unpacking the cars and settling Taija into the apartment, they went out to shop for all the things that they had not packed, like a television! When they returned, Mike hung blinds and curtains while Jeanne and Taija organized clothes.

It had been an exhausting day, and they were all tired. Jeanne had noticed that her daughter suddenly seemed extra quiet. Because Taija's roommate wasn't arriving until the next day, Jeanne suggested that she and Mike stay with their daughter that night. She assured her daughter that they would be fine in the living room for one night. It was not long before they were all asleep, if just from exhaustion.

Jeanne was in a deep sleep when she heard her daughter scream. She awoke, not sure if she had been dreaming, then she saw her daughter's light go on. She went down the hall to find her daughter wide awake and crying. Moments later, Mike appeared at the door. "She's okay," Jeanne whispered. "Go back to bed."

Jeanne and Taija talked for a while, and Taija cried. She told Jeanne that she had not been sleeping. "I know that, but there is no escape from grieving, honey. You have to talk about it. If you try to block it out all day, it will come to you at night," Jeanne said. She sat with her daughter until Taija fell back to sleep. Then Jeanne walked out to the deck and cried.

Moments like those hit Jeanne like a wave. Try as she might, there was no escape from the agony of watching her family suffer and trying to cope with a loss of this magnitude herself. Jeanne was getting used to sneaking away at night, after everyone was asleep, and crying until her whole body hurt. She had convinced herself that if she stayed strong in front of them, it would ease their pain, or at least not add to it. There were times when she felt as if the pain was choking her and she couldn't breathe. She prayed to help her family through this. After a while, she went in and fell asleep, eyes swollen, hands still shaking.

In the morning, they awoke to the sun shining in. That helped too. The rest of the trip was nice, and they kept busy shopping and walking the college grounds. When Mike and Jeanne left for home, their daughter's roommate and friends had all returned to the school. Taija seemed comfortable and happy, and her parents knew her friends would help her through the hard times ahead. Classes were starting the next morning. They said their good-byes, and Mike winked at his daughter. "I'm only a phone call away, baby." She nodded and smiled.

As Jeanne turned the car onto the highway, she glanced over at Mike and saw the tears running down his face. Without looking at her, Mike said, "Do you realize how proud Dad and Guy were of Taija being at Penn State? They wore the shirts and hats all the time. Every time I spoke to my dad, he asked me how it was going for her there. I don't think he could really believe it. He sure always loved that football team," he added, wiping his eyes.

"Yes, I know. Guy texted her cell phone often. It kept her up to date on the family. I know she feels that now, but she *will be* okay," Jeanne said.

Jeanne was comfortable knowing that State College was an entire city of students and staff who all looked out for each other in spite of its size. She knew her daughter was safe and happy there and thought it was the best place for Taija to be right now. Jeanne had also already spoken to the Office of Student Services. She had been told that an assistant vice president of student services would be personally contacting Taija, and she had been assured that they would take over from here. The student service department at Penn State University was second to none, and they were taking a serious interest in Taija's well-being right now.

Taija was contacted almost immediately, on the first day of classes. She was doing her best to avoid a meeting, although she was accepting other help. Then she received a call from the assistant vice president Mr. Joe, who gave her a time to meet him and no hope of backing out. Taija called Jeanne right away, annoyed that her mother had called the school, but she went to the meeting. Mr. Joe addressed the tragedy almost at once. Taija broke down while they talked. Then he took her for a walk around campus.

When Taija called her mother back, Jeanne could immediately hear the difference in her daughter's voice. She heard the excitement and happiness that she had been missing. Taija told her about the meeting and how they had walked around for hours while Mr. Joe showed her, explaining as they went, the art and architecture, two things that fascinated her. She told her mother all the beautiful sights she had seen and the interesting facts she had learned.

Hanging up the phone, Jeanne felt a relief that she had not been able to imagine. She knew what had happened. Mr. Joe had brought Taija's two worlds together—the one at home that she had been trying to block out, the one filled with grief and pain, and the one she loved and was now trying to hide in. Taija could move forward now without trying to separate the two. The burden of hiding was over, and it would be okay. She was not alone, and if she needed someone, she knew where to go.

Life would get better, Jeanne thought.

23

The Larry King Show

September 1, 2009

On Tuesday, September 1, Daniel Schuler took to the airwaves on *The Larry King Show*. With him were his attorney, Dominic Barbara, and his sister-in-law, Jay Schuler.

Mike and Jeanne were watching the show at home.

Larry King started with the introductions and some small talk and a short summary. He mentioned that Daniel and his wife had been in separate cars and that Daniel had taken the dog. Referring to the children, he asked Daniel, "Did you have any concerns about them at all?"

Daniel replied, "Absolutely not. They were with my wife; they were in safe hands."

Jeanne looked at Mike. "Well that's a dumbass answer, knowing the outcome," she said.

Larry asked about the four cell phone calls that were reported to have taken place while Diane Schuler was driving, and Barbara stepped in to answer.

Mike and Jeanne listened to Dominic report his version for a while, not making any sense at all.

Then Larry asked, "So what do you make of all this?"

Jay Schuler answered, "Something medically had to happen. She would never, ever jeopardize the children. We're just confused."

Jeanne stood up. "Okay, I've seen enough; I am not watching these three again. She's confused?"

Mike grabbed her arm. "No, sit down. I want to watch this," he said.

Larry played the piece of the New York State Police conference tape regarding the toxicology in which Major William Carey explained that the report showed that Diane Schuler had a blood alcohol level of 0.19, and a high level of THC, and that investigators had recovered from the van a 1.75-liter bottle of Absolut vodka. When the clip was over, Larry asked Daniel, "How do you explain the vodka?"

Daniel answered, "We usually, we would keep it in our camper the whole season."

Quickly, Barbara interrupted to add, "One bottle."

At the press conference, Daniel and Jay had both said they had *no idea* where the vodka had come from. Jeanne rolled her eyes. "So now he has an idea!"

Jay Schuler interrupted Barbara to say, "Ya know, you have pina coladas, sit by the campfire."

Larry reminded her that pina coladas are not made with vodka.

Jeanne looked at Mike again, saying, "Ya know, booze up, drive into oncoming traffic."

Mike waved at Jeanne to stop talking.

Barbara and Jay interrupted again to explain that this was the bottle from the campsite and the bottle would last all year. "This bottle would last from May until October," Jay insisted.

Jeanne mumbled, "Not this year!"

Larry seemed a little annoyed and asked if they thought the authorities were lying, to which Daniel answered that he knew his wife was not drinking. Larry pushed for an answer, asking them why the authorities would give false toxicology findings, to which Jay answered, "There's an error."

Daniel then added, "There's an error somewhere."

Larry King leaned forward, asking, "It's totally a mystery to you?"

Daniel Schuler responded, "Absolutely."

Larry asked Daniel, "What about the marijuana?"

Barbara interrupted and asked King to stop the drug questions.

Still watching the show, Mike reminded Jeanne that Jay Schuler had initially told investigators that Diane smoked pot *regularly.* Jeanne responded, "Maybe it was an *error.*"

Larry continued even though he had not gotten answers. "Why keep going on?"

Jay answered for Daniel. "You have to understand, Daniel doesn't want the other families to think a drunk driver killed their families."

Jeanne watched Mike stiffen up and slide to the front of the couch.

Larry asked, "What do you think happened?"

Barbara started with his ridiculous theories about blood turning into alcohol, explaining that because the body had been charred, the sugar in Diane Schuler's blood might have turned into alcohol.

Or, Barbara further suggested, perhaps Diane Schuler had had a transient ischemic attack (TIA), basically a mini-stroke, which the medical examiner had already ruled out as a possibility.

Larry asked Daniel about his wife's toothache, and Daniel replied, "She had a toothache for a while, a good two months, but *Dominic knows more about that than me" (*emphasis added).

Jeanne threw her hands up and, looking at Mike, asked, "*H*ow would Dominic Barbara know more about Diane Schuler's tooth than her husband, when she was already dead and buried? The medical examiner's report did not find any such condition."

Mike answered, "You are entitled to a good defense, but if Barbara is outright lying and telling his client to lie, he can be disbarred."

"I can't believe he hasn't been already," Jeanne answered.

Barbara responded to Larry. "She had an abscess on the *right* upper side of her mouth," he said, pointing at his mouth, "about two months old" (emphasis added).

At the press conference, Barbara had mentioned the abscessed tooth but had clearly said it was on the *left* side, but the autopsy report, which had been released the morning of the Larry King broadcast, showed that Diane was missing teeth on the *right* upper portion.

Mike looked at Jeanne and said, "I can see they received the autopsy," to which Jeanne just shook her head.

Jeanne and Mike listened as Larry read a statement from the Longo family.

"Way to go, Joe Longo! That was *really* nice," Jeanne said, looking at Mike when the statement was done.

"That was great," Mike answered. "They're good people."

At one point on the show, Barbara announced, yet again, their plan to exhume Diane's body, a decision that they had apparently made five days after the family received the autopsy report but had yet to do.

"Yea, right. How many times do you think we will hear that? Irving is right; they will never exhume the body," Mike said.

As the show was ending, Jay Schuler stated that they were looking for answers so Diane could rest in peace. Larry then asked Daniel if he had anything to say to the other families, to which Daniel responded, "A drunk driver did not do this to your family."

At that, Mike jumped up in a fury. His face was red and twisted in anger. "Did you hear that?" he asked, not waiting for an answer. "That's what he has to say!"

"I told you not to watch," Jeanne said quietly. "I had a feeling this would not go well." Jeanne could see how upset Mike was. "Do you really think that went well for him? How many people do you think could really be that stupid?" Jeanne was trying to keep Mike calm. "She can't keep track of her own story. Apparently, they forgot they spoke with the police before they got a lawyer. It doesn't change anything. 'She's just confused,'" Jeanne said, mimicking Jay Schuler.

"I just buried my family, and his message to me is that a drunk driver didn't do this?! Does he think I didn't read the toxicology report, that I think he would know more than the medical examiner? Now I know he's covering up, because you'd have to be totally desperate to go on national television and make that much of a fool out of yourself." Mike was furious.

The phones started ringing. Everyone in Mike's family, and everyone else who called for the next two days, would be outraged and insulted.

Jeanne grabbed the house phone. The first call was from Roseann. She was angrier than Mike. Jeanne listened and then tried to calm her down. "Well, I think Larry was okay," she said. "He asked some fair questions; they just didn't answer them."

"Didn't answer them? They just outright lied right on television!" Roseann said, her voice raised.

"Well, apparently you are allowed to lie now, as long as you're not under oath," Jeanne answered.

As they discussed what they had just heard, Roseann agreed that Daniel Schuler looked worse than he had before, but she was still angry—fuming might be a better word.

"I hope they do exhume the body, and then they can get a hair sample, too," Roseann stated.

"They know that too; that's why they probably won't ever really do it," Jeanne said. "The blonde said Diane can't rest in peace yet. Is she kidding, what about the seven mortal sins she took with her? She can't rest in peace now or ever, and with all this lying going on, neither will the rest of them."

The next day, Irving Anolik would respond on NBC, "Daniel Schuler is either an absolute liar or else he is trying to perpetrate a hoax in this matter."

Mike felt a little better.

24
Late-Summer Nights

It was one of those late-summer nights that had become very familiar to Jeanne. The house was relatively quiet, too quiet. She walked out to the patio to find Mike leaning over the pool fence, staring into the woods. It was obvious that he was upset. As Jeanne approached, without turning his head, Mike said, "There should have been a grand jury." He looked at her with the swollen eyes she was growing accustomed to seeing. He looked tired and drained.

"Absolutely," she said.

"I feel like I should have tried harder, insisted. I believed what I was being told, and I trusted that," Mike said, wiping tears from his cheeks. "The DA should not have closed her case after only two and a half weeks. It should have been automatic to have a grand jury. There was no reason to rush and close the case. Seven innocent people died. I bet if it had been the district attorney's brother and father, there would have been a grand jury."

"You couldn't have changed it. It's your nature to trust people; you believe in the system. Unfortunately, the system doesn't always work, but the state police are still investigating. There was truth in every rumor those reporters heard. I believe someone was trying to keep things quiet; I'm just not sure why," Jeanne said.

"They should have called for a grand jury as soon as the Schuler and Hance families hired lawyers and stopped talking to the investigators, just based on the way the investigation was going and the amount of deaths," he said with tears running down his face.

"I agree. After speaking with Jeanine Pirro, I have no idea what really went on. She held that same office for fourteen years. If she said it should have been done and could have been done, I believe her. She thought it should have been done immediately. It could be as simple as it was an election year, or they thought they couldn't prove it, to some complex cover-up," Jeanne said. "It doesn't matter; you know this is far from over." Jeanne couldn't count the nights that she had found Mike this upset. Tonight it looked as though he was deep in depression.

Mike's cell phone rang; he didn't even look at it. Jeanne saw that it was his brother-in-law Joe. She handed Mike the phone, telling him who it was. He answered, and Jeanne went inside. Mike stayed on the phone for a long time. After the initial crying that she had heard, Jeanne saw Mike laughing. Joe was a good brother-in-law and a better friend. His call had come at a perfect time. He was hurting too and trying to keep his family together, but he seemed to know when Mike needed him. Talking to someone who knew what he was going through was really good for Mike.

When Mike got off the phone, he seemed much more relaxed. He told Jeanne some of the things Joe had said, laughing as he said them.

Some nights, that was all it took.

25
September Calms Down

September started to quiet down. The grandchildren had to return to school, and the adults had decisions to make—decisions about the house, the investigation, and the legal proceedings. It was an extremely hard time because the tragedy was still so fresh and the loss was overwhelming. No one seemed to have the strength or desire to proceed with anything. Mike, Roseann, and Marge were still reeling from the shock. It seemed harder each day rather than easier.

Jeanne was worried about Mike. He was devastated, and the kids could see that. She arranged for a doctor's appointment for him. Reluctantly, he went. His health was good, and the doctor took the time to speak to him about his own personal tragedy and to explain what steps Mike could take to help with the overwhelming grief. He had not been able to sleep and barely ate. Jeanne was relieved to see that Mike felt somewhat better when he returned home. It was a start.

Later that day, Jeanne's brother-in-law Brian, called. He had excellent tickets to the upcoming Yankees game and wanted to take Mike and Isaiah, along with his own daughter, Alexa. Mike was happy to accept. He really needed a day to escape the constant loneliness he felt and the never-ending phone calls. What better way than a Yankees game!

Mike had selected a few of the collector comic books that had been his brother's to give to Brian. He thought Brian would appreciate some of the old names that they had all rushed out to buy when they were kids and comics were the rage.

Sunday came and they all met to go to the game, Brian, Alexa, Mike, and Ike. It was the first time Mike and Ike would see the new stadium, and the Yankees won against the Baltimore Orioles! Ike had the time of his life, watching the game at field level. It was a great time. After they returned home, Jeanne was relieved to see an incredible change in Mike, no matter how temporary. At least he could still enjoy life. He was excited for the first time since the accident. He told her that it had felt good to be back in the Bronx. He talked about all the games he and his brother had watched from the subway platform as kids growing up in the Bronx. They were memories he cherished, especially now, and he was grateful for the day out.

Later, Jeanne's sister Carolyn called to see that Mike and Ike had arrived home okay. Jeanne told her what a good time they had and asked her to thank Brian. Ike had come home sporting a new white Yankees cap. "It was a great day for the two of them, and it brought back really good memories for Mike. I think that was really good for him now," Jeanne told her. "Maybe it will replace some of the nightmares."

"Yes, Brian said Mike seemed to really enjoy himself and that they all had a great time," Carolyn said. "Leave it to the Yankees!" She laughed.

"Yeah, those damn Yankees!" Jeanne laughed.

26
Hance Police Tape Released

October 2009

October started with another wild story from Thomas Ruskin. He claimed to have more proof that Diane Schuler was not drunk. On October 18, Ruskin came out with the Tylenol gel cap story. Ruskin claimed that an attendant at the Sunoco station in Liberty remembered Diane had come in weeks before asking for Tylenol gel caps, proving that she'd had a toothache. More than likely, if she had asked for a pain reliever, it would have been for a hangover. All the Sunoco video showed when it was released, however, was Diane wandering around the coffee bar aimlessly, twirling her hair, wearing the same dark sunglasses she had kept on in the McDonald's video, then mumbling something as she *passed* the counter. At no time did it show the attendant even look at her. This would be the same attendant who had *refused to speak with the state police investigators.* There was no audio on the surveillance tape. The video surveillance showed that Diane Schuler was in the store for only twelve seconds. Thomas Ruskin appeared on news shows stating, "We now know that Diane Schuler was attempting to purchase Tylenol or Advil gel caps."

We don't know that, and we don't believe it either. With all that Absolut vodka and marijuana, why would she want a pain reliever!?

In mid-October Mike and his two sisters were meeting at the attorney's office. Attorney Brian Sichol had represented the family early on. The DA's office had forwarded him the CDs of the calls placed to the authorities by the Hances on the day of the accident. When the Bastardis' arrived, they went over some estate paperwork, and then Brian asked if they wanted to listen to the recordings, which they did. Brian's assistant put the recordings on, and she and Brian left the room. As the CD started, Mike, Roseann, and Marge sat and listened intently. Mike looked at the computer screen and noticed that the CD was time-stamped. As he read the times, he realized the calls he was listening to had all been placed *after* the accident had occurred. He jumped up and pointed to the computer, telling his sisters to look at the screen. He rushed out of the room and into Brian's office, where he announced the discovery.

Brian and his assistant went in and looked at the computer, restarting the CD. They were surprised to see that what Mike said was accurate. The calls, which they had also discovered were not to 9-1-1 as reported, had been placed to the Tarrytown police, and the time stamp showed that all the calls had been placed after 1:40 p.m., after the accident had occurred. Mike, Roseann, and Marge just looked at each, and Marge's eyes started to tear. Mike shook his head while looking down at the floor.

A mix of emotions flooded Mike, but the anger was taking over. He lifted his head and looked at Brian. "All this talk of the family making a 9-1-1 call as Warren Hance rushed to the find the van, and just as I suspected, not *one* call was made prior to the crash. These sketchy reports, the limited information, not cooperating with the investigation, all to cover this up. Now it is clear to me: Warren Hance tried to find his sister, brought his father with him to drive her car back, clearly because he knew she was drunk, and *deliberately* did not contact the police because he wanted to find her before the police did. They never called the police until he realized he couldn't find her."

"Listen to the tape. Even the friend that is calling is asking the police if they know where there is a rest stop in Tarrytown. Not once did they say there is a drunk on the road with a van full of children; they were going to keep looking," Roseann said, furious.

Mike stood looking at them with his hands in his pockets. He walked over to the table, pointing his finger on the surface and speaking to Brian. "I want the phone records from the Hances' cell phones and their house phone. They want to meet my family? They will meet my family when they're sitting under oath."

The following week, the Hance police tapes were released to the public through the media. The CD recordings were copies and did not show the public the time stamps as the copy from the DA's office had.

For Mike, it seemed like only yesterday that he had gotten that fatal phone call about his father and brother. Life was not moving on; he was still waiting for answers. He had heard that the tapes had been released, and he turned on the computer to listen.

As he had known, there were no 9-1-1 calls. The caller was identified as a friend of Jackie Hance. The friend was calling the Tarrytown police, asking if the police knew where any rest stops were near the Sleepy Hollow/Tarrytown sign. The caller continued to calmly make light of the situation, later saying it may be a medical emergency, while eight people already lay dead at the scene. The call had come in at least ten minutes *after* the accident. The caller stated that Jackie was "flipping out."

In the set of calls, Warren Hance could be heard—after the accident had occurred—standing in the state police barracks in Tarrytown and asking them to *now* help locate his sister after he had stopped to pick up his father, driven up from Long Island, and then looked for his sister. Standing there at the state police headquarters, and never mentioning that his sister was drunk, Warren can be heard in the background calling Daniel Schuler on his cell phone to find out what cell service Diane had. At one point, he was clearly annoyed and asked Daniel, "Are you with me here, Dan?" This added to the Bastardis' belief that Daniel was probably high also. Again, Warren never alerted police to the fact that the woman who had already killed seven innocent people was drunk, or even that she might be.

Hearing the calls did clear up some questions for Mike and his family. Because Jackie had never talked to the police and Warren had given two different statements, it had not before been clear if Jackie had suspected that Diane was drunk when Warren had gone to look for her. These tapes confirmed that Jackie must have suspected and that there never had been a 9-1-1 call as had been previously reported. No calls from the Hance family had been made to the police until *after* the accident was over. The belief that Jackie Hance may not have known until after the accident disappeared. The Bastardis' hope that Jackie would be the one who would eventually come forward to shed some light on the events of that fateful day was now gone.

Jeanne shook her head. "All that time, I believed Jackie was left totally in the dark. Now I find that she also had a warning—a chance to react too." She repeated what Irving had said, that in all likelihood, this was typical of Schuler's lifestyle and not something that suddenly occurred that Sunday and never before— well maybe her driving drunk was routine for these people.

"The caller said that Jackie was 'flipping out.' What was she flipping out about if she *didn't* know?" Mike said. Then he asked, "Why don't you call my sisters, see if they listened."

"You mean how many times have they listened?" Jeanne replied, dialing the phone. "Hi, Marge, I guess you heard the tapes were released?"

Marge was her usual quiet self. She was struggling with the loss, and every time some news broke, it set her off again. "I'm trying to come up with a reason, any reason why she didn't call 9-1-1 the moment she heard Diane and heard her children crying in the background. Even if her husband told her to wait, I can't understand why she would listen to anybody and not just call 9-1-1. Those were her children," Marge said, stunned. This was something she wanted to understand, and yet that was not possible. "I would never have waited. I would call while he was driving. I would have called 9-1-1 the second I suspected and not have waited for him to get home." She was referring to the reports that said when Warren came home, Jackie had told him Diane was "out of it" and that she could hear her kids crying in the background.

"Marge, the phone-call story has changed so many times, I don't know how you can keep up with it, but we know now that Jackie was aware of the situation before the accident. Don't forget there were at least two hours of phone calls, and who really knows who took the calls. Witnesses saw Diane vomiting on the highway in Orange County the same time the calls were being made." Jeanne said and then added "The same time they had calls from her."

Marge sighed. "I really don't know what to think any more. It just keeps getting worse. Hold on, Joe wants to talk to you."

"Hey, Jeanne, you heard the tapes are out?" Joe asked.

"Yes, I certainly did. I guess we know why Jackie Hance isn't talking to the police either," Jeanne answered. "I wonder if they all realize that when Emma read them the sign, she was only a few feet away from the police, right on the bridge!"Jeanne added.

Joe was not the least bit surprised. "I told you she would have come out talking by now. I'm telling you, it wasn't the first time she was driving drunk, and this time, she was in their car."

"Warren stood in front of the police in Tarrytown and said she might be ill, never mentioned drunk. At the hospital, same thing. She was drunk when she was calling them. I think he's been lying about those phone calls since day one." Jeanne was disgusted. "That is the unfortunate reality, whatever the reason. It looks like he sure didn't want the police to get to that van before he did," Jeanne answered.

"Yeah, the police were at his disposal all day. If he thought his sister was sick, it would be all the more reason to call 9-1-1. I think they had been through this before with different results. Why didn't she try to call Daniel if she was sick? It's a bunch of lies and a cover-up," Joe said.

"It's *pretty interesting* that Warren never called Daniel earlier either. Why wouldn't he have tried to reach him? If everything seemed normal, he should have thought that Daniel would be closer, or still driving, maybe he could get to his sick wife sooner. Why keep that from her husband, especially if he had just been with her? I think she called Warren drunk and rambled on about her husband and whatever was going on. He knew he couldn't call Daniel," Jeanne said.

"Probably, did you want Marge again?"

"No, tell her I'll talk to her later."

27
The Oprah Show Rocks!

October 27, 2009

Oprah was doing a show on the Taconic Tragedy and mothers who drive drunk. Thomas Ruskin, Mike and Jeanne Bastardi, and Elizabeth Spratt from the Westchester County medical examiner's office were all attending via Skype. The show was prerecorded before a live audience and aired on national television about three days later.

The segment started with a pictorial of the accident and narration giving the details. As the video recap of the accident started, it was obvious to Jeanne that Mike would have a really hard time. He had been on a few news shows, short and sweet. While he had been on them, the studios had kept the monitors covered and, if need be, had let him take a break. Mike had not really seen all the pictures Oprah was showing, at least not in a pictorial like this; live in front of an audience. The lead-in to Oprah started, and on came the headlines and the pictures. Jeanne thought it was an excellent presentation, but sitting next to her husband, even without looking, Jeanne could feel him tense up. Mike's face was pale, his eyes were looking down, and he was rubbing his hands together.

Then Mike had to listen to Thomas Ruskin, the Schulers' private investigator, speak.

Oprah first addressed Ruskin, stating that Daniel Schuler continued to deny that his wife drank and asking Ruskin what Daniel believed happened. Ruskin answered that Daniel didn't know but was convinced that alcohol and pot weren't the cause.

Jeanne glanced at Mike, knowing it would be hard for him to listen to this with an audience watching.

Oprah asked Thomas if vodka had been found in the car. When Ruskin said yes, Oprah asked him to explain that. Ruskin went into a story, saying that Diane carried the bottle of vodka back and forth for Daniel because she was frugal and Daniel might want a drink. Oprah questioned Ruskin's explanation, and he continued a lengthy answer, contradicting Daniel Schuler's statement to police—among other statements.

Jeanne half smiled at Mike, trying to stay calm while wanting to scream, LIAR!

Oprah then asked Ruskin how big the bottle of vodka was, and Ruskin answered, "I don't know, because the bottle was broken. My understanding is it was a liter."

Oprah pushed him, saying that you can determine the size of the bottle by the pieces of the glass, and Ruskin answered, "I believe it was a regular one-liter bottle."

Jeanne tapped Mike's leg and smiled. The size of the bottle had been all over the news, and even a bad detective would have known that. *What a seasoned liar*, Jeanne thought.

Oprah moved on, asking Ruskin what he was basing his information on, because the official police report had not been released. Ruskin answered that he had conducted countless interviews, 53 to 57 people, and he went through his story of events.

Jeanne looked at Mike again, thinking, *Countless is right. I didn't see any on the preliminary police reports.*

Oprah asked Ruskin, "How do you, as an investigator, explain the high levels of marijuana?"

Ruskin answered that he couldn't explain the level and wanted to determine if the results were correct.

Oprah continued to say that the Schuler family obviously didn't believe the report, and Ruskin answered that the family believed something else caused Diane's death.

Oprah responded that many people believed Daniel was in denial, and Ruskin answered that his evidence thus far had not shown that Diane was drunk. He continued to tell a story about the phone calls, stating that at 12:08, Jackie Hance had spoken to Diane and everything was fine, adding that it was inconceivable that someone could consume 8 to 10 ounces of vodka and metabolize it in 48 minutes.

Jeanne felt her pulse quicken and looked at Mike while thinking, *It* is *inconceivable. She was most likely drinking all weekend and all day; there were six ounces undigested in her stomach, and two police witnesses saw her vomiting on the side of the road between 11:30 and 11:45. Not to mention the phone call conversations would never be verifiable.*

Finally, it was Jeanne and Mike's turn. Again, they watched the narrated pictorial that had played before Ruskin was interviewed. Then Oprah asked Mike how he was doing, and Mike answered that he was okay, then he added, "Any and all statements Mr. Ruskin has to say about this case, my case, I discard."

Oprah asked Mike, "I heard you think Daniel is covering up?"

Mike answered, "From the beginning when he refused to talk to the state police, denied alcohol, denied drugs, refused to speak about drugs, the vodka was in the car, the marijuana had to be in the car. If you have nothing to hide, you come forward. Seven innocent people have been killed."

Jeanne saw Mike struggling for words, looking down and not able to answer. (That would later be edited out for television.) She asked if she could speak. Oprah told her to go ahead.

After three months of listening to these crazy excuses, Jeanne felt the words just pour out. "I heard Mr. Ruskin say this is the evidence; *nothing* he said is evidence. There are no recorded cell phone calls, no voice mails. As far as the McDonald's video, we were told they didn't notice anything. "The Sunoco video—how a clerk would remember three weeks later that a woman asked for gel caps? What we saw was a woman that at 10:20 a.m. left five children alone in a van—a van that contained a 1.75-liter bottle of vodka—and stroll into the store; the outstanding mother. What is outstanding is that she got back into that van, managed to hold a steering wheel, an almost-–2-liter bottle of Absolut vodka, a cell phone, and marijuana and continue on a four-hour charade that inevitably killed seven innocent people. The cell calls in between is what we want to uncover; were there adults that knew she was very intoxicated and neglected to call 9-1-1. The state police have assured us, had that happened, they would have issued an Amber Alert and maybe we wouldn't be here today," Jeanne said.

The next guest was Elizabeth Spratt with the Westchester County Medical Examiner's Office. Oprah started by telling Elizabeth that Daniel said the report was wrong. Elizabeth responded, "It's 100% correct, no chance of error. We did a lot of work; we have standards and controls; we check and re-check. I stand behind everything we reported."

Oprah asked Elizabeth if there was any question that it's the wrong body or the wrong DNA, and Elizabeth answered, "*No*, no question."

Oprah asked Ms. Spratt if they had tested for other drugs, and Ms. Spratt answered, "Yes, over-the-counter drugs, drugs of abuse, over 300 drugs in every person. Everyone else was negative, on the people in that crash."

From the corner of her eye, Jeanne saw that Mike was listening intently and looking better.

Oprah asked Elizabeth what she thought of Schuler's disbelief, and Elizabeth said, "I'm sad for the whole tragedy, but I know the results are accurate. Many samples were taken, not just the blood samples—the vitreous humor, which was even higher, gastric contents, brain, urine—they all match the alcohol level in her blood."

Oprah asked Elizabeth about the different levels and to explain them. Elizabeth explained that Diane Schuler's BAC was "0.19% alcohol—0.08% is considered intoxicated— it was more than double. A lot of marijuana, high levels of THC, so we know it was more recent—113ng/ml."

Oprah asked her to explain that in layman's terms, and Elizabeth stated, "Usually we would see numbers like 2, 3, 5, 7; this was 113."

Oprah looked astonished. "That, we understand!"

After listening to the rest of the segment, Mike was calm and composed. Oprah went back to him, asking, "When you hear that number, what do you think?"

"Disgusting. I want to remind everybody, Mr. Ruskin said he interviewed 53 to 57 people; not *one* was under oath—not one!" Mike answered

Mike and Jeanne were now off air.

It had all happened fast, and Jeanne and Mike were both trying to analyze what had just gone on. The station crew told them it had gone well and explained how to disconnect and pack up the equipment.

Three days later, the show aired on television. Mike and Jeanne watched from home with a few friends and family members. When the show ended, the silence in the room was evident. The house phone started to ring as soon as the show ended. Jeanne didn't want to answer. Mike took the first call; a friend from Florida was calling. She had loved the show. More calls brought the same reaction. Jeanne was relieved; she had not been sure how the family would react. They were reacting the same way she had: *How dare they lie for that woman, twist the facts, and offer no actual evidence?*

Jeanne was still reeling from hearing Thomas Ruskin speak. She was shaking her head. "His evidence doesn't show she was drunk? Is he a forensic medical expert, did he have new tests done, exhume the body?" Jeanne was furious. "This man is a pathetic liar."

Mike's sister called. "He knows everything but the size of the bottle?" Marge said. "I'm happy that Oprah pushed him on that! You can't lie on her show," she added, laughing.

"That's why everybody loves Oprah!" Jeanne answered. "There are a lot of people that still believe if they hear it on the news, it must be true, and that bothers Mike. It's inconceivable to metabolize that amount of alcohol in 48 minutes? That *is* the whole point, you can't change the truth. She was drunk all day, probably woke up that way," she added

"That whole McDonald's story—he didn't mention she kept her sunglasses on and walked away holding two large sodas," Marge added. "I saw the video."

"Or that he interviewed the McDonalds' witness *seventeen* days later. What a memory! I'm happy if they remember to put the fries in my bag," Jeanne said, "and if they do forget, they don't remember you from two minutes before, when you walk back in."

Roseann was on the three-way call. "What about the vodka bottle story? Do you realize how many of them have changed that story? I love the woman from the medical examiner's office. How much clearer can it get? She really knew her facts!"

They talked some more about the show, more calls came in, and Mike was feeling better than he had in weeks, maybe months. The one-sided defense had been taking a toll on him; he finally had been given a chance to respond the way he wanted to.

28

Phone Bill Mystery

November 9, 2009

Mike was starting to feel better. And he was on a mission. He was not going to stop until he knew exactly what had happened to lead to the deaths of his father and brother. He wanted to know every detail of Diane Schuler's weekend— who was with her and at what time. Who saw her and when. Where and when she had gotten the vodka and the marijuana. How often she had drunk and smoked pot; how often in front of children. Whom she had spoken to that Saturday and Sunday, what they knew, and who could have tried to stop her. More importantly, how much of a role Daniel Schuler had played.

Mike had received copies of Diane Schuler's cell phone bill from the DA's office and had spent hours analyzing it. He was trying to find answers to what really happened that day...*the day his family died.*

He tried to line up the phone calls with the different statements made to the police investigators. He had heard about a 12:08 cell phone call with Diane Schuler and had heard Ruskin state on Oprah's show that the call was with Jackie Hance. From everything the family had heard, no one could deny that Diane should have sounded drunk on a phone call at 12:08. Mike had to find a record of this call.

A reporter called Mike to discuss the bill. When he asked Mike what he thought about the 12:08 call, they discovered that the call did not appear on Mike's copy of the bill and neither did a few other calls, calls between 11:30 and 12:08, though they were all on the Verizon copy of the bill. The call had been placed to Diane's cell phone from the Hance's home phone. *Was it left off my copy accidently?* Mike wondered. Maybe, but doubtful; that was a huge oversight. It was the most important call on the bill, considering the time frame. Mike also confirmed that no calls had been made to Daniel Schuler and that he had not called his wife's cell.

Just who was actually speaking to whom? No one will know for sure unless a civil suit is filed, and that still might not answer those questions. Once a suit is filed the attorneys might be able to subpoena other phone records or other records that might help shed some light on the entire weekend. Analyzing the different versions of phone calls is interesting, at least.

Warren Hance had given the state police investigators two *different accounts* of the cell phone calls, changing whom he claims to have talked to and when, and what was said. What the Verizon phone bill does show is that three calls were placed to the Hance home, one call to Warren's office, and two calls to Diane's cell from the Hance home. The first call is made at 11:33 am.

Looking at the police statements and the Verizon phone bill, Mike can assume that both Jackie and Warren spoke to Diane before 1:00 p.m. Diane would have clearly been heavily intoxicated and high by then, according to the toxicology reports. According to medical experts, she would have sounded drunk to anyone who spoke with her. The phone bill showed several misdialed numbers, which, the investigators had theorized, had been a child trying to dial. The other calls had probably been placed by Diane, as the numbers were in her speed dial. It was just a tragically sad story. At 1:02, Warren made an eight-minute phone call to Diane's cell. That is a long call, eight minutes. Had someone dialed 9-1-1 right then, maybe the Taconic Tragedy would have had a different outcome. At that time Diane's van was parked directly across the highway from the state police in front of the Sleepy Hollow/Tarrytown sign that Warren claimed Emma read to him, and where the cell phone was later found. The state police could have walked over in less than one minute.

That knowledge will haunt Mike for a very long time.

29
No Proof of Error

November 2009

In the natural order of life, we bury our parents. No matter what age a person is, it's never easy. You may think you expect it, you may think you're prepared, but when it happens, it's devastating. You bury an entire generation. It's like losing your connection to the past. When it's your father, you bury the head of the family. In Mike's case, he lost his only brother at the same moment. You're never prepared for that; it becomes overwhelming.

Imagine that when you are finally told the circumstances that a drunk driver has killed your loved ones, a million emotions and questions flood your mind. You wait for the details, for the answers that can explain their fate, but those answers never come. Instead, your family watches as several news channels air the family of the drunk driver praising her, excusing her, saying the medical examiner has made a mistake—the autopsy, the toxicology report, the witnesses have all been in error. Enter the attorney and the private investigator who fabricate story after story, whose investigation "has not shown that she was drunk." Imagine this added to your grief.

Of course there is no reasonable answer and, more importantly, *no proof of error.*

After the district attorney announced that no criminal charges would be filed, the Sunoco video and a still photo from McDonald's were released to the public. As if to add insult to injury—or, rather, murder—the Schuler lawyer and private investigator continued the fantasy with absurd excuses for Diane Schuler while the family continued to portray her as the perfect mother—compared to the perfect murderer, maybe.

It appeared they had a goal: damage control. The story was too horrific and the pictures too gruesome. The police investigators had said more than once that the families were not cooperating, so now Diane's family had the dilemma of portraying this killer mom as an innocent victim of some unknown disease, at the victims' expense.

On November 18, Mr. Ruskin arrived at another theory, the Chicken Selects theory. According to this theory, Diane Schuler was able to place a complicated order at McDonald's that fateful morning so she must have been sober. He said that she was so "engaging" that she was able to persuade the cashier to place the order before lunch. He continued to say that she talked to the employees at length and even called a manager over.

The actual McDonald's video, which will not be released for public viewing, merely shows Diane Schuler walk in, order food, pay, and walk away—no long conversation, no negotiating, just standing there, wearing her dark sunglasses for the entire visit and walking away holding two large cups, not the size that comes with kids' meals. The state police obtained only one witness statement from McDonald's—from the register employee—short and sweet. It never mentions the negotiations. The statement was obtained 17 days after the accident. In addition, Thomas Ruskin was aware that the public would not view the McDonald's video, so he was free to lie about it, but the Bastardi and Longo families and their attorneys have viewed the video.

Thomas Ruskin had no real proof that Diane left the campground sober. The videos had little to offer. She never falls down in them, but that doesn't mean she was sober or straight. In watching the videos, the Bastardis' thought she looked dazed and confused, seemed odd with the dark sunglasses indoors. It was all interpretation. The Schuler entourage was not looking for new medical proof, just talking about it— suspicious, at least.

30
Thanksgiving

On the day before Thanksgiving an article came out in the newspaper that said one of the victims had survived briefly—the driver of the trailblazer, Guy Bastardi. Mike and Jeanne's daughter was arriving home from college for Thanksgiving and Jeanne was horrified that she might see the article about her uncle. There had been some questions pertaining to the release of information, information being leaked to the press. The bigger problem was who could handle the press and how they could stop all the phone calls Mike was receiving. The media attention was making life chaos. For much of October and November, while the media had been throwing around all the theories about Diane's innocence, the Bastardi family had been discussing the possibility of hiring additional civil attorneys—and possibly also investigators—just to combat the stories being put in the news. With this article's release, they knew it was time

By the time Taija arrived home for the holiday, Mike and Jeanne had quietly banned all newspapers and news channels from their home. Thanksgiving was quiet; no one really knew what to do or had the desire to do anything. Mike's sisters and their families went out to dinner in Yonkers. They chose a nice Italian restaurant that would be serving a traditional Thanksgiving dinner. The meal was very good, but for Roseann and Marge, it only served to remind them of what they were missing—a big family Thanksgiving dinner at their parents'. It would have started with the escarole soup that Mike Sr. would have made and would have then been followed by the homemade manicotti that Guy would have insisted on. The house would have been filled with family and friends stopping in along the course of the day. Long tables would have stretched through the dining room, and Grandma would have decorated for the holiday with the kids in mind.

Jeanne and Mike had dinner at home. Jeanne's sister Carolyn, several of Jeanne's nieces, and a few friends joined them. Carolyn had brought trays of food that her local deli in Wappingers Falls, *Deli Supreme*, had thoughtfully provided. It was delicious, especially because no one had really felt up to the task of cooking.

After dinner, Jeanne asked her nieces Alexa and Amanda to each pick a doll from the collection that had been her mother-in-law's. The dolls had come home with Mike. He and his sisters had divided the collection that had been their mother's. She had collected dolls for years and had had an entire room devoted to displaying them. It was fascinating to look at them all. Every doll was in perfect condition. After much thought, each girl decided on her favorite. Dessert followed, with an abundance of small talk while football played in the background. Somehow, they had a relatively pleasant day.

Later that night, after everyone had left, Jeanne found Mike outside. He was facing the backyard, but she could see his shoulders moving. She didn't have to see his face to know what was going on. She walked out and ran her hand down his back, asking, "Are you all right?"

Mike turned, wiping his eyes. "No, not really. That news article…I keep visualizing my father that day, looking ahead and screaming, 'Watch out,' and then it was just over for him, but I know my brother. I know how he must have tried to turn and look at my father. When that accident happened, if my brother *was* alive, I know he turned his head and saw my father gone and then realized he was dying too." Mike was crying harder. "And I have to hear her family praise her, defend her, lying, making up excuses? I *really* can't take it. I don't care what they claim Diane Schuler was before; I *know* what she was the day she killed my family," Mike said.

The next morning, Jeanne started to research, hoping to find a lawyer who had handled cases of this magnitude. She was worried about Mike; he was not doing a whole lot better. She wanted an attorney who would relieve Mike of some of the pressure he felt. Mike wanted this to end with some answers. He just had more questions.

Jeanne contacted the office of John Q. Kelly. She spoke to John Kelly a couple of times, explaining the situation. On Christmas Eve, John and Mike would finally touch base. John would ask Mike what he expected and tell Mike what he thought he could do. When Mike hung up the phone, he would sound almost excited, definitely relieved. He would call Irving and his sisters. Mike would set up a dinner meeting with Irving, John Kelly, and his family. Already, Jeanne could see that Mike was more relaxed, as if a huge burden had been lifted.

31
Thomas Ruskin Exposed!

December 7, 2009

In early December the call Mike had been waiting for finally came. It had been confirmed that Thomas Ruskin president of CMP Protective and Investigative Inc., the private detective for Daniel Schuler, was a convicted felon—the man whose ludicrous remarks through this whole ordeal had tortured Mike. The man who had made up his own theories and gone on numerous talk shows to say he had found no evidence that Diane Schuler had been drunk. He had come up with the Tylenol gel cap theory, the Chicken Selects theory, and several other ridiculous ideas that had been painful for Mike to hear, all of which had prolonged the agony. He had been trying to excuse that woman from murdering Mike's father and brother.

According to federal court documents, "Thomas Ruskin was indicted in Louisiana in 1996 on a twelve count federal indictment, charging him with several felonies including 'defrauding various commercial airlines.' After being forced to resign from the NY Police Department, he later pled guilty in 1999, to a single federal count of conspiracy. He was sentenced to five years of supervised release (probation), ordered to pay restitution of $9,875.00, a fine of $5,000.00

and assessment to the Clerk of the court $50.00. Counts 2 through 11 were dismissed in the plea agreement."

"Makes you wonder about the Sunoco video, doesn't it?" Mike asked.

Thomas Ruskin had obtained the last video of Diane Schuler from a gas station and turned a copy over to the police. The employees of the gas station had later refused to talk to the police.

"It makes me wonder about every single word and every single witness. I always wondered about the video. She wandered aimlessly around the coffee bar, never stopped to ask anything, and then pulled out on two wheels, cutting cars off. What about all these witnesses he claims to have spoken to, or what he claims they said?" Jeanne answered, "How do you know any of it is true? The police don't have these names or statements, or at least they're not in police reports." She was getting angry as she spoke. There were time lapses in the video, and now they didn't know if those were intentional or not. "How does a convicted felon get a license as a private investigator, or a gun permit?" she asked.

"He might not be licensed; he never actually uses the word licensed, and I have no idea if he carries a gun," Mike answered.

"Amazing. I guess we can safely rule out ethical. There should be a disclosure law for that. A client has a right to know that before they hire him. These people put their trust in him and then find out he's a convicted felon, a disgraced cop—that's not right." Jeanne was shocked. "Call your sisters; they're all going to flip."

"You get them on the phone." Mike said.

Jeanne dialed the phone and got Roseann, who got Marge on a three-way call, and then Jeanne told them the news.

"You have got to be kidding me! How do you know this? I cannot believe this is possible," Roseann said. She was furious.

"Are you sure about this? How can he get away with hiding that?" Marge asked.

"It is definitely true and it has been confirmed. The papers are being faxed to us." Jeanne said.

"Ruskin has handled evidence and questioned witnesses. Does Irving know this?"Roseann asked.

"Yes, of course," Jeanne said.

"What about the district attorney. Is she aware of this?" Roseann asked.

"I am not sure, but I don't think she knows yet. I don't see that she could, under the circumstances. There would have to be a cred-itability issue, or at least I would hope there is," Jeanne said.

"I want to know how someone like that gets a license as a private detective and works on sensitive matters like this. He could be out there covering the whole story up," Roseann said.

"I have always thought he was hired to cover up, not investigate. What was there to investigate? The toxicology report? They have not retested any tox results! " Jeanne said.

"I don't really know, but it seems like some kind of oversight, or it should be," Marge said.

"His website said that he worked for the Clintons. No one would have checked his background?" Roseann asked

"I have no idea about that or when he worked for the Clintons; I do know he was initially indicted on twelve charges of crimes against the US Government, which would be a big security oversight. I'm sure if Hillary knew, she would not have let go of her briefcase!" Jeanne said.

Jeanne listened while the other women ranted. Then she said, "So now we know; Thomas Ruskin was a dirty cop, obviously not a very good criminal, and it's not looking too good for his private-detective skills, either! Seems like a pretty good liar, though."

The *New York Post* ran the story the day after Mike received that call about Ruskin. Irving Anolik was quoted in the paper as saying, "The credibility of Thomas Ruskin is severely impaired by the fact that he is a convicted felon in the federal court in Louisiana."

32
Lawsuit Filed

December 10, 2009

In early December, Mike, Roseann, and Marge accompanied the attorneys to White Plains and filed the civil lawsuit. The lawsuit named the estate of Diane Schuler, and Warren Hance, the owner of the vehicle, and is open to amendments.

While they were exiting the courthouse, where a few reporters waited, a reporter from a major news network approached Mike. "Have you heard that Daniel Schuler has checked into a rehab?" she asked.

"Well, you're the second person to tell me that," he replied.

"We can't confirm that because of the medical privacy laws."

"I don't have to confirm it, and I'm not at all surprised," Mike answered.

Sometime in late November or early December, Mike's family had heard that Daniel Schuler had gone into a rehab center. They had also heard that the babysitter had moved into the house. Neither had come as a surprise. The investigators and some of the reporters had been following this. It might be true and it might not, but it hasn't been ruled out. For Mike and his family, this information could make more of the puzzle pieces fit.

Of course, another private investigator would give his unwanted opinion. While Roseann, Marge, and Mike were on their way home from filing the lawsuit, Michael Archer made a statement on the news saying that it was "in poor taste to sue Warren Hance at this time of year."

That rattled Roseann and Marge. "Did you hear what Archer said on the news?" Roseann asked Jeanne when they had returned from court.

"Yes, who cares?" Jeanne continued, "Seven people died at the hands of a drunk driver who happens to be Warren's sister. She was driving his van. The Hances have already opened an estate account for their girls in anticipation of either suing or being sued, so I'm sure he anticipated a lawsuit."

"It just ticks me off; we had no control over that," Roseann said. "The holdup was having to file to get an estate attorney for Diane Schuler because her husband had not bothered to set up an estate," she said, referring to the fact that previously, one of the Bastardi-family attorneys had had to file for an executor to oversee the estate of Diane Schuler. The court had appointed an administrator for her estate.

"Archer worked for the *defense* of Joran van der Sloot in Aruba. All of a sudden, he has morals! Was he worried about the Holloways' holiday season?" Jeanne could not have cared less. "Eight people are dead. Inevitably, that will make this time of year harder. The lawsuit had to be filed; nothing pertaining to it starts now anyway. He's not a lawyer; what would he know about that? Why would you even listen to what he says?"

"It is just nonstop. It starts to get to me. Every time I turn on the news, something else comes on about my family," Roseann said. "I have had to tolerate this for months. How can we ever start to move forward when we can't even get away from the news?" Her eyes were starting to tear, and her lips quivered.

Jeanne could see that this was taking its toll on Roseann. The grief was hard enough to bear; the antics in the news were unnecessary and hurtful. "Focus on all the good and caring people you have heard from in the last few months; in the end, they are the only ones that really matter," Jeanne answered.

33
Christmas

Christmas was rapidly approaching whether or not the Bastardi family was ready. For weeks, Mike and his sisters had been emptying their parents' house. Mike had taken most of his brother's Christmas decorations. Like his parents, Guy had loved to decorate for Christmas. The children had always been fascinated by all the animated figures he had. This would be the first Christmas that had not been celebrated at Mike's parents' house. It had always been so festive, crowded with people and an abundance of food and desserts, all homemade, which would have taken days to prepare. Most of the grandchildren had never been anywhere else and when they were young had thought that Santa went only to Grandpa's house. It was where they mailed their letters to Santa. They were all clueless about how to proceed this year.

Not knowing how Mike would feel, Jeanne had suggested that it would be nice to put Guy's Christmas tree in their living room. It was a beautiful seven-and-a-half-foot artificial that you had to touch to believe it was not real. Mike had agreed, and he and Ike had set the tree up, putting Ike's favorite animated figure next to it. As expected, it was done with mixed emotions. When the tree was up and all the white lights lit, it looked beautiful. Ike was so happy that he was anxious to continue decorating, but Jeanne could see it had been more than Mike could take right now. She suggested that they get some of their Christmas boxes from the attic and start to look through them. That satisfied Ike for the night.

The following day, Jeanne took Ike to pick out a real tree. He chose a nice big one, and when they returned home, they set it up in the family room. Jeanne filled this one with colored lights, and they hung decorations all over it. They put out Christmas linens and some fresh wreaths and garland. Then they surveyed what they had done. It looked nice, festive but not overdone. Jeanne asked Ike if he wanted to set up Uncle Guy's Lionel train around the tree and surprise Mike.

"No, I don't think Dad will like that," Ike answered, looking sad.

"Sure he will," Jeanne answered. They set up the train, which was surprisingly heavy.

When Mike arrived home, Ike showed him what they had done, starting with the family room, which was traditionally where they put the Christmas tree. All the Christmas colors had come to life in this room. Then he walked him to the living room where the train ran on the tracks under the tree, with lights on and whistles blowing. Mike looked inside the room; the tree looked beautiful with just the white lights and the train under it. His eyes were tearing.

Ike looked at Jeanne. "I told you he wouldn't like it."

Mike grabbed his son's shoulder. "No, I love it, Ike. Thank you."

Christmas came and went quietly. Absent this year were the wonderful holiday traditions that the family had come to know over the years, such as homemade pasta, dinner, and dessert served in the same traditional Italian style. It would start with the antipasto, salad, and bread. Next came the soup, then the pasta, which was always homemade and took days to make. Dinner would include two different meats and a variety of side dishes, followed by nuts, fruit, and an amazing variety of sweets. More important than the meal were the smells that filled the house for days and everyone in the kitchen cooking together. Like a well-oiled machine, everyone had known their roles in the kitchen. It was hard for them to imagine that it would ever happen that way again and even harder to imagine that it wouldn't.

Jeanne and Mike stayed home with their children. Jeanne's sister Carolyn and her daughters, a few of Jeanne and Carolyn's other nieces, and a few of Taija's friends joined them. They opened gifts and enjoyed a nice Christmas dinner followed by a variety of desserts. It was a nice, relaxing day and had gone better than expected. With the fireplace and both trees lit, the house had a real country-Christmas feeling, yet it was a change from the busy Christmas that would have taken place at Mike's parents' home. That would have been very festive, crowded with people, and filled with excitement. Opening the gifts from Guy was usually the best part. He'd had impeccable taste and gone to great lengths to find the perfect gift for each person. His nieces had been overwhelmed with Coach handbags, jewelry, Ugg boots, or whatever the hot item had been that year. No one was more thoughtful shopping! The kids would have had piles of gifts to open from their grandparents. Mike's parents had always thought that was important; his mother would have shopped throughout the entire year and then spent days decorating the house.

Jeanne noticed Mike sometimes standing in the doorway and staring into the living room at his brother's tree, but he never actually walked into the room. *All in due time,* she thought.

Roseann and Marge had decided that their families would get together at Marge's house. For most of their children, this would be the first time that they had not had Christmas at their grandparents' house. As young children, they would rush over early in the morning, anticipating that Santa had left their gifts there. They had never been disappointed—their grandparents and uncle had made sure of that! The thought of shopping and cooking this year seemed like nothing so much as an unwanted chore, though.

Following mass on Christmas, they all gathered at Marge's. Roseann arrived with a smile, but her red eyes told another story. If not for the children, she would have been happy to forget the day after church. Looking at Roseann, Marge said with a smile, "Oh no, don't get me started." Roseann just smiled at her. They both remained teary eyed off and on throughout the day but managed to put on a happy appearance. The house was crowded as all the kids' friends starting arriving, bearing gifts.

Together, Roseann and Marge had prepared a big and delicious meal, and just feeding that many took up most of the day. Everything went smoothly as they kept the conversation light and comical. The dessert hour, which took more than hour, was filled with a delicious variety of pastries, cakes, pies, and cookies. It was the time the children really enjoyed. Grandpa's rule had been to allow them all to try whatever and as much as they wanted to taste. That had never changed.

34

Justice Not Served

January 2010

Plenty of investigative reporters, private detectives, and others were calling Mike with information. Most people were not comfortable with the way the investigations had gone. There were certain things that were not adding up or making sense. What had been the rush to close the investigation after less than three weeks? Half the people involved had not been interviewed.

Mike remembered Irving saying things such as, "fragrance of criminality" and "The ingredients for disaster were already in her car." Knowing the type of attorney that Irving was, Mike hung onto these thoughts and they replayed through his mind.

The alcohol news took a long time to release after the police press conference; that was information that should have been discovered almost immediately. The results of the toxicology report were clear. Mike and Jeanne had also spoken to other medical examiners, including one of the country's most respected forensic experts. Others had weighed in on television talk shows, on the news, and in news articles. They all agreed that with blood alcohol at that level, Diane Schuler would have been clearly drunk to any listener.

Between the Bastardis' and their attorneys, they had spoken with several district attorneys, former, current, and some running hopefuls. They had *all* said they would have called for a grand jury for varying reasons, including just relieving themselves of the responsibility. This had been after all, the worst accident in Westchester County in 75 years.

Daniel Schuler worked under the Nassau County Police Department, yet he had not even been drug-tested after this. He was ignoring requests to give his own hair sample. If he had really wanted to clear his wife's name, he would have cooperated with the police and given his own hair sample. He chose to hire an attorney who has been known to represent less-than-upstanding clients. Other rumors swirled about the Nassau County Police Department's involvement and its connection to both Hance and Schuler. Warren Hance had not been forthcoming with the police during his investigation. He had continued to tell the police that his sister wasn't feeling well, on both the day of the accident and the days following. The tapes that were later released had told another story, however. In addition, the New York State Police had been denied access to the families.

Tom Ruskin, a private investigator for Schuler, had obtained the Sunoco video and had given a copy of it to the district attorney, who had entered it into evidence. Those same people from Sunoco refused to speak with the police, and it is now known that Ruskin is a convicted felon. The Sunoco video had 90 seconds of gaps. According to the video, Schuler spent *only 12 seconds* in the store, and yet he created a whole story from that.

Dominic Barbara had free rein to say anything he wanted without proof. At the initial press conference, he stated that the campground owner Anne Scott, said she saw Diane Schuler leave that morning, kissed her good-bye, and smelled her alcohol-free breath. An online news video later showed Ann Scott stating that she had never said she kissed Diane, did not even know her that well, and had no idea why Barbara would say that. Tom Ruskin had been the private investigator for Barbara at the camp and had stood at the press conference behind Barbara, never correcting him.

More than one reporter suggested to Mike that there might have been some kind of cover-up from the beginning. The story kept changing, no one had been put under oath, and half of the witnesses were never really questioned, and yet no grand jury was called. Diane Schuler's husband and brother had immediately retained attorneys and were not cooperating with the police; there are not many reasons people do that. These reporters believed that Hance and Daniel Schuler both had something to hide, something that required having attorneys and lying. Nothing about this seemed to add up or make sense.

No one had expected the story to get this big; maybe that's why it had.

Justice had not been served.

****

In early January, Mike and Jeanne, Roseann and Bobby, and Marge and Joe, along with Irving and his wife, met with John Q. Kelly for dinner. John had handled many high-profile cases and was familiar with the Taconic story. Mike made his position clear: he wanted the answers he had sought from the beginning.

The Bastardi family retained Mr. Kelly. In January, John Q. Kelly filed to amend the lawsuit.

35
Life Goes On

February 2010

Life goes on, or at least that is what they say. It didn't seem to be going on for the Bastardi family. If the morning was good, the afternoon wasn't. If the afternoon was, the evening wasn't. Then there were the nights—the long, cold February nights. They had made it through the holidays and were anxious for warmer weather and better days.

It had taken months for Mike and his family to empty the house, and that had been a painstaking ordeal. Forty years of memories had to be cleared away. One day during the emptying process, Mike had arrived at the house in Yonkers as two men were starting to move some of the items out and load them into a truck. Marge had watched Mike as he walked downstairs into Guy's apartment. She had seen him open a draw in Guy's dresser. Immediately, he had shut the draw and put his head down and started sobbing. It broke Marge's heart to see her brother in so much pain. She knew that memory would stay with her forever. Her eyes had filled with tears as she had quietly gone upstairs, wondering how they would survive this tragedy.

The house still contained all of their late mother's belongings in addition to those of Mike Sr. and Guy. Just watching Mike carrying in boxes was an emotional chore. He had mixed feelings about anyone touching their things and felt guilty doing it himself. He packed each item with incredible care. Watching his sisters struggling through this chore made it that much harder for him. He wanted to take away some of their pain, but he knew he couldn't. At the end of every day, he had been emotionally drained. It had been the same for his sisters, maybe worse. Everything they had seen was something worth saving. Everything had a special memory. Every day, someone had broken down. It had been a long and emotionally draining process.

They were at Grandpa's house on one of those days. Looking around at how empty it was, they found it hard to imagine that this was the same house that had held so many happy memories. All the wonderful times they had shared there seemed to fade with the emptiness. They sat at the table, holding coffee in paper cups bought at a deli. Even the coffee pot was gone now.

Jeanne looked at Marge and Roseann. "I hate coffee in paper cups," she said, tilting the cup. "It takes the taste away."

Roseann looked at her cup and nodded. "Did you hear about the Hance Foundation?" she asked.

"No. A foundation for what?" Jeanne asked.

"It said to honor the memory of the three girls that died in a tragic car accident," Roseann said.

"A tragic car accident?" Jeanne put her cup down and looked at Roseann. "You mean a tragic homicide committed by his sister. What cause would this money be going to, Mothers Against Drunk Drivers?" Jeanne asked.

"Various things, to help less-fortunate children. There is a website for the foundation. It seems that they have catered birthday parties for the girls, sport events, other fund raisers. Warren and Jackie are very involved, they make a lot of public appearances for the foundation."Roseann said.

"Say no more." Jeanne said holding up her hand. The three women sat silently, and then Jeanne said "Losing your children is by far the worst thing that can happen to anyone, but how can you move forward if you really don't know the circumstances of their deaths?" "Considering the situation, I'm not so sure that the foundation isn't more about the Hances than the children."

"What do you mean?" Roseann asked.

" I cannot overlook the fact that they never really cooperated with the investigators. It seems suspicious because Warren Hance has always acted suspicious. I think the girls should be remembered, but it strikes me as a little odd. No mention of the other little girl?" Jeanne asked.

"No, just the three Hance girls," Roseann answered.

"That's sad."Jeanne said

"I don't know what they were thinking that day," Marge said.

"I have no doubt that they were good parents or that if Warren was the one leaving the campground with Diane that day, there would have been a different outcome, "Jeanne said. "Nevertheless, no matter what their intentions were that day, it backfired in a big way, and seven innocent people died, not three."

"I know what you mean. If Warren thought it was a stroke, it gave him more reason to call 9-1-1," Roseann said. "At least someone should have."

"Warren not coming forward has kept Daniel Schuler from possibly facing charges, maybe even himself. At the least, after he knew his children died, he should have come forward. Frankly, he had nothing left to lose. You saw that when Jackie Hance's police tape was released." Jeanne was adamant. "Until they tell the police what really happened that day, to me, it just shows they all have something to hide. This has also destroyed life as we and our children all knew it. The difference is, we had no warning," Jeanne said.

"Sooner or later, they will have to answer for that. People will always see what went on. That will always make people wonder. I don't believe that a person can go on indefinitely keeping something like this inside," Marge said.

"They can if they keep busy. If you lie long enough, you start to believe it. Go back and read the newspapers in order. At the initial police conference, the state police captain said she contacted her brother *two hours* before to say she wasn't feeling well. That is what Warren Hance *initially said*, before he knew his children were dead. He was playing games with the police. How many investigators and medical people have said it would have been almost impossible not to know that she was drunk? Read it in order: Hance hires attorney, Hance refuses to speak to police, family not forthcoming.

Warren and Jackie have been all over? If they were able to start a foundation, arrange these events and parties, appear all over in public and Jackie can speak out in public, why isn't she able to give a statement or answer questions for the police? They can put themselves in the limelight but they can't answer questions about why they are there? Let's try to be real here," Jeanne said.

"There must be an unbearable pain in losing your children—it's unthinkable—but he should have cooperated more and relieved some of the agony that the rest of us have had to go through," Marge added, her eyes showing the strain of sitting in the empty house. "He should have wanted the same answers."

"He already had them, Marge, and he continued to lie about it," Jeanne said. "Warren Hance should have been honest the first day. There is a reason he didn't call 9-1-1, and it's not because he panicked. Panic doesn't last for hours. His sister murdered his children while he was driving around trying to find her before the police could find her; that is what happened," Jeanne said. "The question is why he would not have fully cooperated with a homicide investigation, not if he is sorry now. His wife waited, too, and whoever else was at the house that day. All the foundations in the world can't change what has already happened or what has been taken away," Jeanne said.

"Well, if they never talk to the police, it seems like that would be true," Roseann said. "They could have talked to them at any time. It is hard to forgive."

"Don't lose sight of what really happened here. You were at the same DA meetings as I was; you spoke to the same investigators. Nothing has changed. They are all the same people that we were told were liars then, and they're still lying now. They obviously didn't care what Mike or anyone else was going through. They sat back while he had to endure the Anbesol, the Chicken Selects, the stroke, the perfect-mother crap. No apology, no anything. Having to grieve while this freak show tortures him, kills your father and brother, and then makes a *mockery* out of it! What kind of people do that and hide from the police? People who already know the truth. I have no reason *not* to believe that. The Hances don't speak to Daniel Schuler. Why?" Jeanne was not willing to excuse the Hances' or Schulers' behavior. "As far as I'm concerned, Warren gave Barbara the fake-illness defense; he said she wasn't feeling well, and he never changed that lie. It all stemmed from that," Jeanne said.

"Well, I agree that after he heard his children died, he should have fully cooperated with the police and told them everything he knew. There were four calls Sunday and one Saturday night too. If something set her off, he knows what it was and he probably would know when she was drinking," Marge said.

"He knows exactly what happened; he chooses to hide it. Not calling for help and lying about it? LYING about it! Why did Warren tell the police he had his wife call 9-1-1 as he left the house? That never happened. Why didn't he call? That never happened. He knew that day to lie about it, but he didn't know to actually call? Are you kidding me? Running around patting yourself on the back is an outrage. *His children suffered, that's who suffered.* Are you so sure that a nine-year-old wouldn't have told her father her aunt was smoking pot or stopping the car to vomit? Nine-year-olds know that; if he even really talked to her. I am heartsick for those children, but I can't feel sorry for him; Warren obviously only cares about Warren. People forget, that's what they count on; over time, no one will remember the actual events. He has allowed my husband to suffer terribly; I can't feel sorry for him," Jeanne said angrily. "Of course there is nothing worse than losing your children, but minus a nervous breakdown, I don't excuse not talking to the police, and we can see Jackie has not had one. If they have kept Daniel Schuler from criminal charges, then shame on them! I don't know how they live with it. I would not stop until I knew everything about my child's last weekend. The whole weekend," Jeanne said.

"Well, I can understand that. I feel the same way as Mike. It stays with you, the always wondering, the worrying about the next nasty insult." Marge sounded incredibly sad. "It has never been very fair."

"No one should have to deal with that in the wake of such a tragedy. No one!" Jeanne said.

36
The Following Spring

March 2010

March arrived, and they were another month closer to spring. The winter had been cold, and a blizzard had crippled Mike and Jeanne's town for two days. March 20 would have been Guy's fiftieth birthday. His sisters had arranged for a private service at the cemetery. A priest from St John's would offer a reading and prayer.

The family all met at the cemetery. The weather was warm and sunny for March, and the abundance of flowers was beautiful. Walking down the sidewalk, Mike stopped to look around. The cemetery was always meticulously kept and the site laid out in perfect unison. "Can you imagine the birthday Guy would be having today with this weather? They would have been cooking for days. He would have loved that," Mike said with tears starting to cloud his eyes.

Jeanne nodded. "Yes," she answered quietly, forcing a smile. "He would have loved that."

This was the first time the younger children had been to the cemetery since the funeral. Mike watched his nephew Joey walk up with his little girl, Brianna, who was holding a balloon. Joey helped her tie it to the flowers that had already been placed. As Joey and Brianna walked away, Mike heard her say, "Daddy, I am gonna miss Uncle Guy's meatballs forever."

Smiling, Mike whispered to himself, "So am I."

The service was lovely, and when it ended, Mike walked over to thank the priest. Jeanne watched as they spoke privately for a while. Jeanne could see that the priest was reading a Bible passage to Mike. When Mike returned, he seemed more at peace. Whatever questions he had asked, he felt satisfied with the answers.

Jeanne and Mike joined the others for lunch at Marge's home. It was a small luncheon. They made sandwiches and ordered in pizza.

"How are your kids doing, Marge?" Jeanne asked.

"Better, I guess. Richie and Jenna were really hovering around me for a while. Jenna and I can talk about it now. Richie still won't talk. He keeps everything inside. At the mere mention, he just gets teary eyed and walks away. He was so close to Grandpa," Marge said.

"I know. The therapists for Ike told us early on that it was just too traumatic for kids. It takes away all sense of security and stability. Kids anticipate who will be next," Jeanne said.

"What about your kids, Jeanne?" Marge asked.

"Same as yours. I don't think any of them will ever really get over it, but they'll learn to live with it," Jeanne said.

"I know," Marge answered. "It has changed the way they will all perceive things."

"What about my brother, Jeanne; how is Mike?" Marge asked.

"Better. He has had to tolerate a lot. He wants justice and he doesn't feel like he has gotten that," Jeanne said.

"Well, I can agree with him on that," Marge said.

"I know, Marge; you have all been to hell and back," Jeanne said sympathetically, then added "It's not over yet, Marge."

37
Always More News

March 2010

On March 12, the Oprah episode on which Mike and Jeanne had appeared aired for a second time.

On March 23, 2010, *Newsday* reported that the family of Diane Schuler was awaiting the results of new toxicology tests, hoping to prove that she had not been drunk and high when she had killed seven people and herself. Samples of Schuler's blood and other fluids had been turned over to NMS Labs, a state-certified firm, confirmed the Westchester chief medical examiner. Schuler's husband had vowed to clear her name.

Thomas Ruskin of CMP Group said the lab was retesting for alcohol and drugs and ensuring there had been no lab mix-up. Ruskin stated, "The results are due in a short amount of time; we are being methodical."

Dr. Hyland, Westchester County's chief medical examiner, said that the Schuler family had waited long enough to ensure that the results would differ. The samples degrade over time, the doctor stated, and there would be a reduction in all the drug results.

Ruskin claimed that the Schulers would make a decision about exhuming the body after the tests were completed. Dominic Barbara said of exhuming the body, "That's one of the things that are going to be happening real soon."

The next day *Newsday* reported that Mike Bastardi Jr. called for the body to be exhumed and a hair sample to be extracted, to see how much of Diane Schuler's drug abuse could be found. A six-inch strand of hair can detect drug abuse going back a year.

Of course, no test results were ever released to the public, nor was the body ever exhumed. This had become a story of deceit, and no one had expected the results to be made public.

38

Easter

In April came Easter and the first sign of spring. Jeanne and Mike were having his family for Easter dinner, the first holiday that they would all be spending together. The weather proved to be cooperating after a long and snowy winter. Marge and Roseann made a visit to the cemetery, bringing flowers, and then headed upstate with their families. Taija was home from college, and Carolyn and the girls were also coming. Carolyn was bringing some vegetarian dishes that Taija loved. She was an excellent cook and always came up with exotic dishes that everyone enjoyed.

When Carolynn and her daughters arrived, Alexa looked at Taija's Easter basket and said, "Mom, I told you she would have a basket."

"Jeanne, you made her a basket?" Carolynn asked.

"Yes, why? I put age-appropriate things in it, and I didn't make her hunt for eggs," Jeanne answered.

"I thought my girls were too old, so I wrapped their things," Carolynn said, laughing, "and I think they wanted baskets."

"That is the same basket my mother-in-law gave Taija for her first Easter. I have used it every year," Jeanne said adding, "I couldn't stop this year."

"Wow, I can see that. They don't make them like that anymore!" Carolyn said, looking over the basket.

The rest of the family arrived, and they greeted each other and sat down for some small talk, bringing each other up to date on their most recent family news. Easter had always been a big family holiday filled with tradition. No one really knew what to expect today. They were trying to start new traditions and keep the spirit up, yet at the same time, they all had that empty feeling in the pits of their stomachs. The day continued with a pleasant and delicious dinner, a variety of foods both traditional and vegetarian. The women had previously decided to try to do things a little differently this year. There was much talking and laughing during the meal. The absence of mentioning Grandpa and Guy was obvious to them all and they struggled to keep the silence of their loss.

The day went smoothly. The men went off to play some golf while the women talked. Bob was an avid golfer, and Mike enjoyed golf as well. Joe could just plain power hit! They were all surprised to see how well Mike's son could already play at his age. He had been playing with Mike for a few years as well as taking lessons, and he had quite a good, strong swing.

The women discussed the torment of emptying the Yonkers house. Jeanne showed her sisters-in-law the silver that had been their mother's. It had been found buried in a cabinet, and when Mike had brought it home, it had been black. Jeanne had spent hours carefully cleaning and polishing each piece. Marge and Roseann were surprised to see it looked like new. They looked at some of Guy's collectibles that were displayed in a separate cabinet and at some pictures that Mike Sr. had put together. In dividing the items, the women had been surprised to find that each of them had a room, or at least part of a room, that resembled their parents' and brother's home. Roseann and Marge discussed the importance of the items that they had each chosen. Memories just poured out—some with a little sadness but most with fondness. It was a relief to finally mention their lost family members today. It was hard to believe that they were all gone now.

The cousins went off to take a walk. It seemed as if the accident had brought them closer together. In spite of all the support that they had from others, they now shared the bond of disaster. They had more of a need to be together. Without having to speak, they knew what the others were feeling—that lonely, empty feeling that could erupt into tears at any given moment. They seemed happy today, and there was a lot of laughing between them. It was nice for the adults to see them together.

Dessert followed: a variety of desserts that all the women had brought filled the long table. Then came the usual conversation over weight as they all sampled the platters. Everyone seemed relaxed and cheerful. It was a good day. The first signs of spring had that effect on people.

Of course, they always had some news headline to keep them amused, even after the holidays. In May, Dominic Barbara made headlines. He was arrested for violating a protective order and was charged with criminal contempt after he walked into a bagel shop and sat down with his estranged wife while she was having coffee with a friend. He had gone in with a police officer, claiming that his wife was stalking him. Two days later, *he* was arrested.

After reading the story about Barbara, Mike called his brother-in-law Joe and asked him if he had read the article. Joe answered, "I heard it on the news. What the hell kind of people are we dealing with here?" Joe was laughing.

"I know what you mean," Mike said, also laughing.

39
Father's Day

It was a beautiful Sunday morning in June, and Mike's son awoke early, knowing that it was Father's Day. He was anxious to make a surprise breakfast for Mike. Jeanne and Ike went downstairs early to get started and let Mike sleep. Jeanne poured coffee while Ike started gathering the food. He grabbed the bacon and looked at his mom. "I don't know if Dad likes turkey bacon," he said, looking nervous.

"Yes, he likes it; it is healthier, too," Jeanne answered.

She also was anticipating how today would be for Mike. As they were preparing breakfast, Mike came down smiling. Jeanne was relieved to see how happy he appeared. Their daughter, home from college, came down soon after, which was early for her. Jeanne figured they all wondered how the day would be.

Breakfast was a success. It seemed like ages since they had all sat down to breakfast together. Ike was happy to have helped cook and served his dad breakfast. He was anxious to have Mike open his gifts, and of course the gifts from Ike were golf related.

The day proved to be nice and quiet. Everyone sat by the pool, barbecued, and enjoyed the sunny weather. Mike hit golf balls with his son. He wore the new outfit that his daughter had given him. Everyone seemed happy.

Jeanne was surprised at how many calls and text messages Mike received wishing him a happy Father's Day. Family and friends from all over had thought of him today, and she was happy and grateful for that. It had kept him in good spirits. It was also important to Mike because it meant that they had also remembered his father and brother. He spoke with his two sisters; they would be stopping at the cemetery and then getting together in Yonkers.

Later that night, Jeanne went upstairs to check that Ike was settled for the night. He had school in the morning. When she came back downstairs, she saw Mike leaning on the pool fence. As she approached the patio, she could see that his shoulders were moving up and down. Her heart ached for him. All day, he had kept his sadness inside for the kids. She walked outside and put her hand on his trembling back. He looked at her, and with tears streaming down, he said, "I still can't believe it."

40
Reconstruction Report

June 26, 2010

The New York State Police released the reconstruction report on June 26, 2010. The report showed that Diane Schuler had been driving at 85 mph and Guy at 74 mph at the time of the crash. The report neglected to include the witness statement from the person in the black SUV that had been driving in front of Guy and witnessed the accident in his rearview mirror. It also neglected to mention the dozens of witness statements that reported Diane speeding by or that the black box only recorded the last five seconds of Guy's speed.

Having possession of the other reports, the Bastardi family was able to see all of that information. To them, Guy's speed at the time of the accident was irrelevant. He had been sober and driving in the right direction. Maybe he had sped up to get out of the way. They will never know.

The state police had also released the first 9-1-1 calls from July 26, 2009. So, of course, to further add to Mike's pain, they heard from Michael Archer again: "Six people had the ability to swerve out of her way and call 9-1-1." That was almost the most ignorant statement yet. Those first six calls had come from the people on the exit ramp that Schuler had entered the wrong way. She had hit the Trailblazer as she had come around a corner which, to the drivers going the right way, was a blind turn and a slight incline. Several cars moved at once to avoid her but at 85 mph in the wrong direction an accident was inevitable. Using Archer's way of thinking, there should never be another head-on accident anywhere even when a drunk driver drives 85 mph down a parkway in the wrong direction, with a van full of children. Simple, just get out of the way.

Mike was furious, and that anger spread through the family quickly.

Roseann called Mike's house. "Is he saying its Guy's fault for not getting out of the way? Has he even read the police report?"

"He is just another Ruskin," Mike said, "just ignore him."

"Well he's probably leaving for Peru; van der Sloot has been arrested for killing a girl this time. He'll be more useful there," Jeanne said, laughing. She could not have cared less about Archer.

"What do you mean?" Roseann asked.

"Yea, remember he was part of the defense for van der Sloot when the girl went missing in Aruba," Jeanne answered. "Now there is a girl murdered in Peru and van der Sloot was arrested as the main suspect. This girl's family is prominent in Peru, and they are not letting him get away this time."

"Are you kidding me?" Roseann asked.

"No, it's true; check the news." Jeanne answered.

"Because everyone has to voice their unwanted opinion," Roseann answered.

"It's their claim-to-fame wish. People like that have no idea the pain they inflict on others. Just keep in mind no one else cares what he says either," Jeanne said.

"It's amazing the people we have had to deal with and the things we find out about them," Roseann said.

"Yeah, like a recurring nightmare" Jeanne said.

41

One Year Later

Almost a year had passed since the Taconic Tragedy, which had drastically changed so many lives. The house in Yonkers, which was now just a painful reminder to Mike and his family, was put up for sale. The grandchildren had seemed to grow closer; one had graduated high school, one was engaged to be married, one had finished another year of college, one was starting kindergarten, and two were moving into middle school. They relied on each other during their bad days, like a secret club that one had to be a member of to understand.

The adults still struggled; grief has a way of drawing out a person's anger, and it seemed to go back and forth like an emotional roller coaster. They supported each other, but their focus turned to getting the answers that they all still waited for—especially Mike. The loss had hit him tremendously hard. He had suffered for the entire year, but time has a way of making people see things more clearly.

The Schuler family had maintained Diane's innocence, with no proof to dispute the findings. The Hance family had remained quiet, kept their information to themselves, and gotten on with their lives.

The difference now was that Mike was no longer willing to accept excuses. He never really had, but now he was stronger and more determined for answers. He was pushing for the civil suit. He wanted the answers that he believed the Schulers' and Hances' already had.

Like the rest of his family, Mike didn't believe a word that Daniel Schuler or his family said. Mike had his own theory. He believed that Diane Schuler had been no novice to booze or pot, and neither was her husband, Daniel. Mike believed they went camping and drank every weekend—not one bottle a year, but one bottle a weekend. At some point after Diane arrived at the campsite, she had discovered that Daniel had not gone up on Thursday as he had said, but on Friday. Because they were already having marital problems, that discovery had set the tone for a weekend of arguing, drinking, and getting high. Maybe Diane had found out where Daniel really was Thursday night.

On Sunday morning, according to Mike's theory, Diane awoke still trashed from the night before. Daniel had had enough and left, driving away and never looking back and that was why there were no calls between them that day. That was his fatal mistake. Diane had continued on her binge, dragging the children around with her. By 11:30, she had started calling Warren, already trashed and probably telling him the whole story. By 12:08, it had been obvious that she was wrecked. At 1:00, panic had set in for the Hances. Warren planned to find Diane before the police found her, and he took his father along to drive the van back. Jackie waited at home. No one called the police; they didn't want the police to know Diane was drunk. The last fatal mistake. Then had come the crash, eight people dead. Having heard that the van and Diane had been burned, the families may have anticipated that it might go undiscovered that Diane was drunk.

Once the toxicology report was released, Mike thought, both men had realized that they needed lawyers. They had retained attorneys and stopped cooperating with the investigation. Attorney Dominic Barbara had sought the publicity. He had probably approached Daniel Schuler. Barbara had hired private investigator Thomas Ruskin, who had often worked for him. Thomas Ruskin had the job of covering up Daniel's role. The only defense they had been able to come up with at this point was that Diane was not drunk and Daniel had never known anything, leaving her sober at the campsite. Neither Warren nor Daniel could blame the other without showing his own role. Thomas Ruskin had started his ridiculous masquerade, led by Barbara. That show of lies and deceit had continued for the next year.

Mike was willing to wait. Eventually, the civil suit will begin.

In June, Mike and Jeanne's phone started ringing again; reporters wanted to know the plans for marking the first anniversary. The family had planned a private church service and a service at the cemetery, and Mike had wanted to see the crash site for the first time. He wanted to see just how much visibility his brother would have had. He had worked the accident down to the second following the release of the reconstruction report. He had read and reread all the police reports and witness statements and had spent countless hours reviewing news reports, accounts, and information available on the internet. He was ready.

Of course, as they had all learned, this case was full of ugly surprises. On the evening of July 25, Mike received a phone call. Apparently, Dominic Barbara had a news conference planned for the anniversary date—an update on the accident, said Mike's source. Barbara had brokered a deal for Daniel Schuler to sell the rights to exhume his wife's body to a production company that planned to do a documentary. The Bastardis' could only imagine the sympathetic spin Barbara had planned at his conference, but the reality was that there is not one. Daniel Schuler needed money, so the wife he supposedly loved so much had a selling price; she could be dug up, filmed, and autopsied so Daniel Schuler could get some cash. Maybe that was why the previous test results they had done had never been released—there was no money in that, and by now, there would not be much left to autopsy. On television, Barbara announced that Daniel Schuler would be receiving one hundred thousand dollars in exchange for the documentary, which would air on HBO.

It just kept getting worse.

On July 26, 2010, the Bastardi family proceeded with the services and the trip to the Taconic Parkway as planned. Just the immediate family and a few friends attended the church service. A service at the cemetery followed, which included the playing of "Taps." Then they made the trip to the crash site. As the family stood there, Mike tried to visualize the scene from a year before—where his family had ended and where four children had lain on the ground…the scene he had read so much about. He tried to put the pictures he had seen in their places on this highway. The destruction had been devastating. The same questions remained unanswered, and again he wondered why there had not been a grand jury.

With the much-appreciated help of the New York State Police, Mike had gotten the answers he had sought that day. The family placed a cross and flowers where the car had come to rest. It was a sad day, but when it was over, Mike felt more relief than sadness. It had been hard, but he had accomplished what he had wanted to. He was convinced that his brother could not have even seen Diane Schuler coming, especially at 84 mph in the wrong direction.

Dominic Barbara's news conference never took place, and there was never any mention of a service of any kind for the Schulers' little girl, who had also died in the crash. The Bastardis' did hear that Daniel Schuler had been filming that day, though, for the documentary.

Some things were exactly as they had expected.

42
9-1-1 Calls Released

August 2010

It was August 30, 2010, more than a year since the fatal accident. Mike received a call from Fox 5 news, informing him that under the Freedom of Information Act, the news channel had obtained the release of the 9-1-1 calls made shortly before and after the crash. Before they released them to the public, they were giving him the courtesy of hearing them first. He was appreciative and arranged a time.

The news team arrived and sat down with Mike and Jeanne. There were nineteen calls on the tape. The tape started with the first few frantic callers from the exit ramp, next an off-duty New York police officer informed the dispatcher of several fatalities. In seconds, the 9-1-1 switchboard had lit up. Several calls were answered and the callers quickly told that the police were on the way. Mike and Jeanne could hear the frantic calls in total panic, the 9-1-1 dispatchers trying to answer the calls as more poured in, going unanswered. The tape played the sound of phones ringing and people screaming.

As Mike and Jeanne sat and listened, the pain came back, feeling like it had on that fatal day. The first caller announcing the crash brought Jeanne to tears. It was too much of a reminder. She could picture the frantic caller, and she knew who had just gotten hit; a chill went through her whole body. It was hard to listen and not picture the scene. Mike waved to stop the tape. "It's okay, I'm good, and I want to hear all the calls," Jeanne assured him. The news team was patient, stopping and restarting the tape several times. When it ended, they all talked, and Mike gave a brief interview.

After the news team left, Mike said, "That was nice of them. He was a great guy, and I really liked him."

"Yes, he was," Jeanne said.

That evening on the news, Mike and Jeanne watched and listened as Ti-Hua Chang reported the story and played a few of the calls they had heard that afternoon. The calls were still chilling to hear.

Over the next few days, friends and relatives called to comment and to check in on the family. No matter how many times they heard such a tragic story, it always seemed shocking. It brought back the pain, the horror, and the tears and reopened the wounds. Knowing the world could hear the tapes took away any sense of privacy for the victims' families. It was very hard to give up all privacy for such a personal family tragedy. Mike felt a great need to protect his father and brother's dignity, and yet he could not stop the news. The overwhelming support was all he had to get him through it.

The pain stayed fresh.

43
No Closure...

September 2010

On September 1, 2010, Thomas Ruskin publicly reversed his findings. In his televised statements, he stated that he had "found nothing to contradict the autopsy report that Diane Schuler was drunk and high." He further stated that he "was never consulted about the HBO documentary and it had come as a complete surprise."

The information pertaining to the documentary had been discovered on July 26 and had been released publicly. The documentary was already being filmed. Thomas Ruskin's revelation was a little late in coming. They already had the results of the previous samples that had been sent out and retested; they could have released those results publicly months before but had elected not to. After more than a year, exhuming Diane Schuler's body might not have anything to offer anyway.

"I don't believe this guy," Mike said, pointing to the newspaper.

"Sounds like trouble in paradise," Jeanne said.

"Is he kidding?" Mike was furious.

"Looks like Tom didn't get a cut for the body selling. Maybe he's angry at Dan and Dom; it could get ugly, "Jeanne said, smirking. "He was the most publicity-seeking liar of all. Now he concedes to the medical examiner. Maybe Tom has gotten himself in a bind. If they do an autopsy, he'll look that much worse trying to admit it later. What's their plan, act surprised?"

"He has no creditability," Mike answered.

"His timing alone shows that," Jeanne answered.

On September 4, Mike responded to Mr. Ruskin's statement. "We find no comfort in what Mr. Ruskin has acknowledged. Mr. Ruskin, along with Dominic Barbara, and Daniel Schuler have spent the entire year fabricating excuses for this drunk and high woman, ignoring the true evidence that was presented, and with absolutely none of their own. Their excuses were an absolute outrage and insult to all of us. We will do whatever we can in our capacity to prevent them from profiting from the criminal acts of Diane Schuler and will protect the dignity and respect that my father and brother deserve. We continue to search for the answers and are confident that we will find them."

There can be no closure without knowing the truth.

****

After hearing of the documentary and that Daniel Schuler is reportedly receiving one hundred thousand dollars in exchange for selling the right to exhume his wife's body and film the exhumation, the attorney for the Bastardis filed with the court to block Daniel Schuler from profiting from a murder and the criminal acts of Diane Schuler. That is pending.

In February 2011, Dominic Barbara was disbarred for a period of eighteen months, for reasons unrelated to the Taconic Tragedy.

A few days later he abruptly announced his retirement.

On March 18, 2011 The New York Daily News reported that the Nassau County district attorney was probing lawyer Dominic Barbara for swiping money from Daniel Schuler. Recently Schuler had asked Barbara for the $110,000 which had been placed in an escrow account and Daniel was told it was unavailable. Schuler contacted the Nassau County district attorney.

(Thomas Ruskin had claimed for months that the family could not raise a mere $10,000 to have Diane's test results re-done.)

Further investigation into the Taconic Tragedy is ongoing as the Bastardi family awaits the civil suit.

* * * *

The Bastardi's are seeking assistance from the NY State Attorney General's office.

Another year, Another Heartbreak

For another moment time stood still
As a thousand hearts broke and a little boy cried...

Joseph Miller
June 26, 1969-February 2, 2011

Rest peacefully and know that you are so sadly missed
And that I am grateful to have called you my brother-in-law.
Farewell dear friend.

Jeanne & Mike

CPSIA information can be obtained at www.ICGtesting.com
Printed in the USA
LVOW062334250412

279057LV00001B/179/P